BASIC/NOT BORING
LANGUAGE SKILLS

FIFTH GRADE
BOOK OF
LANGUAGE TESTS

Series Concept & Development
by Imogene Forte & Marjorie Frank

Illustrations by Kathleen Bullock

Incentive Publications, Inc.
Nashville, Tennessee

Thank you to the students who contributed works to this book.

About the cover:
Bound resist, or tie dye, is the most ancient known method of fabric surface design. The brilliance of the basic tie dye design on this cover reflects the possibilities that emerge from the mastery of basic skills.

Cover art by Mary Patricia Deprez, dba Tye Dye Mary®
Cover design by Marta Drayton and Joe Shibley
Edited by Jennifer J. Streams and Angela Reiner

ISBN 0-86530-460-2

PRINTED IN THE UNITED STATES OF AMERICA
www.incentivepublications.com

TABLE OF CONTENTS

INSIDE THE
FIFTH GRADE BOOK OF LANGUAGE TESTS

"I wish I had a convenient, fast way to assess basic skills and standards."

"If only I had a way to find out what my students already know about language!"

"If only I had a good way to find out what my students have learned!"

"How can I tell if my students are ready for state assessments?"

"It takes too long to create my own tests on the units I teach."

"The tests that come with my textbooks are too long and too dull."

"I need tests that cover all the skills on a topic—not just a few here and there."

This is what teachers tell us about their needs for testing materials. If you, too, are looking for quality, convenient materials that will help you gauge how well students are moving along towards mastering basic skills and standards—look no further. This is a book of tests such as you've never seen before! It's everything you've wanted in a group of ready-made language assessments for 5th graders.

- The tests are student-friendly. One glance through the book and you will see why. Students will be surprised that it's a test at all! The pages are inviting and fun. Clever, spunky frogs tumble over the pages, leading students through questions and problems. Your students will not groan when you pass out these tests. They'll want to stick with them all the way to the end to see which frog is holding the STOP sign this time!

- The tests are serious. Do not be fooled by the catchy characters and visual appeal! These are serious, thorough assessments of basic content. As a part of the BASIC/Not Boring Skills Series, they give broad coverage of skills with a flair that makes them favorites of teachers and kids.

- The tests cover all the basic skill areas for language arts. There are 24 tests within 6 areas: reading, writing, grammar & usage, words & vocabulary skills, study & research skills, and spelling.

- The tests are ready to use. In convenient and manageable sizes of 2, 4, or 6 pages in length, each test covers a skill area (such as "parts of speech" or "correcting spelling errors") that should be assessed. Just give the pages to an individual student, or make copies for the entire class. Answer keys (included in back) are easy to find and easy to use.

- Skills are clearly identified. You can see exactly which skills are tested by reviewing the list of skills provided with each group of tests.

HOW TO USE THE
FIFTH GRADE BOOK OF LANGUAGE TESTS

Each test can be used in many different ways. Here are a few:
- as a pre-test to see what a student knows or can do on a certain language topic
- as a post-test to find out how well students have mastered a content or skill area
- as a review to check up on student mastery of standards or readiness for state assessments
- as a survey to provide direction for your present or future instruction
- as an instructional tool to guide students through a review of a lesson
- with one student in an assessment or tutorial setting
- with a small group of students for assessment or instruction
- with a whole class for end-of-unit assessment

The book provides you with tools for using the tests effectively and keeping track of how students are progressing on skills or standards:

- 24 Tests on the Topics You Need: These are grouped according to broad topics within language. Each large grouping has three or more sub-tests. Tests are clearly labeled with subject area and specific topic.

- Skills Checklists Correlated to Test Items: At the beginning of each group of tests, you'll find a list of the skills covered. (For instance, pages 10 and 11 hold lists of skills for the four reading tests.) Each skill is matched with the exact test items assessing that skill. If a student misses an item on the test, you'll know exactly which skill needs sharpening.

- Student Progress Records: Page 118 holds a reproducible form that can be used to track individual student achievement on all the tests in this book. Make a copy of this form for each student, and record the student's test scores and areas of instructional need.

- Class Progress Records: Pages 119–120 hold reproducible forms for keeping track of a whole class. You can record the dates that tests are given, and keep comments about what you learned from that test as well as notes for further instructional needs.

- Reference for Skill Sharpening Activities: Pages 121-122 describe a program of appealing exercises designed to teach, strengthen, or reinforce basic language skills and content. The skills covered in these books are correlated to national curriculum standards and the standards for many states.

- Scoring Guide for Performance Test: A performance test is given for writing. For a complete scoring guide that assesses student performance on this test, see pages 130–131.

- Answer Keys: An easy-to-use answer key is provided for each of the 24 language tests. (See pages 124–144.)

THE FIFTH GRADE LANGUAGE TESTS

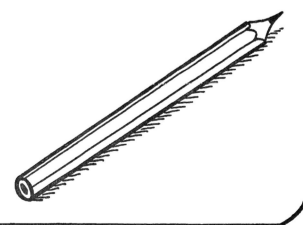

Reading Skills Checklists

Reading Test # 1:

WORD MEANINGS

Test Location: pages 12–17

Skill	Test Items
Determine word meaning from context	1–11
Determine meaning of phrases from context	12–14
Recognize and use synonyms	15–19
Recognize and use antonyms	20–24
Choose the correct word for the context of a passage	25–27
Use knowledge of prefixes to determine word meaning	28–33
Use knowledge of suffixes to determine word meaning	34–39
Use knowledge of root meanings to determine word meaning	40–49
Considering the context of a word, choose the correct meaning of a word with multiple meanings	50–57
Explain literal meaning of idioms	58–70

Reading Test # 2:

LITERAL COMPREHENSION

Test Location: pages 18–23

Skill	Test Items
Identify literal main ideas	1–4
Identify details that support an idea or point of view	5–7
Choose the best title for a selection	8–10
Gain information from titles, headlines, or captions	11–15
Determine sequence of events in a passage	16–17
Read to find details and information	18–31
Make use of graphics to gain understanding of a text	27–31
Read to follow directions	32
Read to find information in a table of contents, glossary, or index	33–40

Fifth Grade Book of Language Tests

Reading Test # 3:

INFERENTIAL & EVALUATIVE COMPREHENSION

Test Location: pages 24–29

Skill	*Test Items*
Identify implied main ideas	1, 4, 5, 11
Draw logical conclusions from a written text	2, 3
Determine the author's purpose or bias	2, 6, 10
Use information gained from a text to make inferences	7, 8, 9, 20–23
Distinguish between fact and opinion	12, 13, 14, 15
Identify cause-effect relationships	16, 17, 18, 19
Use information gained from a text to make predictions	24, 25
Make generalizations based on material read	26
Evaluate ideas, conclusions, or opinions from a text	27, 28, 29–35
Read to interpret charts, graphs, and tables	29–35

Reading Test # 4:

LITERATURE SKILLS

Test Location: pages 30–35

Skill	*Test Items*
Identify plot, setting, and characters of a piece of literature	1, 2, 3, 7, 14
Identify main and supporting characters	2, 3
Identify literary devices and their effects (alliteration, simile, metaphor, onomotopoeia, rhyme, rhythm, repetition, puns, personification, idioms, hyperbole, imagery)	4, 21–42, 45
Recognize characteristics of different literary forms (genres)	5, 8, 48–55
Identify and analyze characteristics of different characters	6
Identify other elements (theme, tone, mood) of a piece of literature	9, 10, 44, 47
Recognize effective use of words and phrases to accomplish a purpose in the writing	11, 12, 13
Identify the literary techniques used in poems	16, 17
Identify the author's bias or feelings about the subject	43
Identify the author's purpose	46

Fifth Grade Book of Language Tests

WORD MEANINGS

Name _____

Possible Correct Answers: 70

Date _____

Your Correct Answers: _____

1. Only a <u>robust</u> athlete would have the endurance it takes to climb to the top of that 200–foot frozen waterfall.

   In this sentence, *robust* means:
   a. strong
   b. careless
   c. experienced
   d. beginning

2. Everyone stared at Frannie, who looked <u>conspicuous</u> wearing her bikini on the snow-swept ski slope.

   In this sentence, *conspicuous* means:
   a. unnoticeable
   b. confused
   c. standing out
   d. up-to-date

3. After falling from the high wire, the performer lay <u>inert</u> for several minutes before lifting his head off the ground.

   In this sentence, *inert* means:
   a. upside-down
   b. tangled up
   c. motionless
   d. alert

4. The full <u>fury</u> of the storm splintered the small sailboat into pieces.

   In this sentence, *fury* means:
   a. suspicion
   b. force
   c. peacefulness
   d. shape

5. A line of extreme skiers, zigzagging and winding their way down the steep slope, left a <u>serpentine</u> pattern in the snow.

   In this sentence, *serpentine* means:
   a. beautiful
   b. treacherous
   c. shocking
   d. snake-like

6. Soon after lunch, Chester was hungry again. He began to regret that he had brought such a <u>meager</u> lunch on his hike.

   In this story, the meaning of *meager* is:
   a. tasty
   b. unappetizing
   c. plentiful
   d. skimpy

7. A young surfer survived so many horrible crashes and near-death accidents that he began to believe he was <u>immortal</u>.

   In this sentence, *immortal* means:
   a. wicked
   b. honorable
   c. able to live forever
   d. motionless

12

On the Track of the Yeti

What an amazing day! I am so lucky to be a part of this <u>riveting</u> experience! Here I am, a <u>conventional</u> kid from Ohio, off on an extraordinary quest to <u>shed some light on</u> the mystery of the abominable snowman. This <u>elusive</u> creature, also known as the Yeti, supposedly lurks in the Himalayan Mountains of Asia. Several groups of explorers before ours have returned without so much as a glimpse of the creature.

For centuries, people have had different opinions about the Yeti. Some believe it is just a myth. Others insist the abominable snowman is real. I'm standing on a Himalayan mountain, <u>my eyes boring through the thick snowfall</u>, trying to find out for myself. In jest, my climbing partner grabs me from behind and growls. As we stand laughing together, we hear another growl— one that sounded much different. We turn to look, and <u>our jaws drop to the ground</u>.

8. In the first paragraph, a *riveting* experience:
   a. is frightening
   b. takes great physical strength
   c. holds someone's attention completely
   d. is complicated

9. In the first paragraph, *conventional* means:
   a. unusual   c. young
   b. ordinary   d. intelligent

10. When the writer's friend grabs her in *jest*:
    a. the friend is fooling around
    b. the friend is very frightened
    c. the friend is about to slip down the mountain
    d. the friend is angry

11. In the first paragraph, *elusive* means:
    a. hard to catch   c. dangerous
    b. extremely large   d. extinct

12. When the passage says that the trip was intended <u>to shed some light on</u> the mystery, it means:
    a. the searchers probably carried flashlights and lanterns.
    b. the searchers hoped to learn more about the abominable snowman's existence.
    c. the searchers would climb only during the daytime.
    d. the searchers intended to take photographs of the Yeti.

13. When the writer says ". . . <u>my eyes are boring through the thick snowfall</u>," she means:
    a. She must use a drill to cut through the thick snow.
    b. The searchers have to dig their way out of the snow.
    c. The Yeti is hidden behind thick snowfall.
    d. Her eyes are staring hard trying to see through the heavy snowfall.

14. <u>Our jaws drop to the ground</u>, means:
    a. The writer and her friend are knocked to the ground.
    b. The writer and her friend dive for the ground.
    c. The writer and her friend are so shocked that their mouths fall open wide.
    d. The searchers have injured their jaws.

Name _____

13

Fifth Grade Book of Language Tests

ADVENTURES, UNLIMITED
Join Us for the Adventure of a Lifetime!

Witness the perils of a grand bullfight.
Face down a menacing dragon with a valiant knight.
Take a precarious climb up the face of Half Dome.
Venture into the world's most colossal cavern.
Dare to face the bizarre mysteries of the Bermuda Triangle.
Challenge the treacherous waters of the Black Tiger River.
Unearth relics of primitive civilizations.

Probe the universe for black holes.
Join scientists to scrutinize Bigfoot's tracks.
The Ultimate Thrill: Bungee jump from the Eiffel Tower!

Read the ad for *Adventures Unlimited.*
Find and write a **synonym** for each of these words found in the ad above:

_____ 15. threatening

_____ 16. study

_____ 17. huge

_____ 18. dangers

_____ 19. search

Read the ad for *Adventures Unlimited.*
In the ad, find and write an **antonym** for each of these words:

_____ 20. safe

_____ 21. cowardly

_____ 22. least

_____ 23. ordinary

_____ 24. modern

Choose the correct word for the context of each sentence.

25. The old prospector had a _____ day, finding five large nuggets of gold before noon.
    a. memorable   c. challenging
    b. uneventful   d. terrible

26. We rolled on the ground with laughter at the _____ sight along the side of the hiking trail.
    a. amusing   c. horrible
    b. fascinating   d. hilarious

27. Weren't you surprised to learn that such an accomplished athlete is a very _____ person who does not seem interested in being in the spotlight?
    a. generous   c. boastful
    b. humble   d. rude

Name _____

Use your knowledge of prefixes to choose the correct word for each definition.

28. carry across a space
    a. export
    b. transport
    c. import
    d. report
    e. deport

29. say something again
    a. reply
    b. explain
    c. restate
    d. discuss

30. beyond human
    a. inhuman
    b. superhuman
    c. dehumanize
    d. subhuman
    e. humanoid

31. having a similar look
    a. uniform
    b. reform
    c. inform
    d. deform

32. having a hundred feet
    a. centipede
    b. decapod
    c. tripod
    d. quadruped
    e. pentapod

33. under water
    a. submarine
    b. ultramarine
    c. marina
    d. marinate

Use your knowledge of suffixes to choose the correct word for each definition.

34. without friends
    a. friendliness
    b. friendship
    c. friendly
    d. friendless

35. person who acts
    a. acting
    b. access
    c. actor
    d. action

36. act of being injected
    a. injection
    b. injector
    c. indigestion
    d. reject

37. cause to be tender
    a. tenderness
    b. tenderly
    c. intended
    d. tenderize

38. able to be loved
    a. loving
    b. lovely
    c. loveless
    d. lovable

39. full of fear
    a. feared
    b. fearless
    c. fearful
    d. unafraid

Name _____

15

Word Meanings

Use your knowledge of the meanings of root words to answer these questions.
Choose words from Frannie's list.

40. Which word or words have a root that means **hang**?

_____

41. Which word or words have a root that means **sleep**?

_____

42. Which word or words have a root that means **hand**?

_____

43. Which word or words have a root that means **work**?

_____

44. Which word or words have a root that means **carry**?

_____

45. Which word or words have a root that means **see**?

_____

46. Which word or words have a root that means **move**?

_____

47. Which word or words have a root that means **write**?

_____

48. Which word or words have a root meaning **sound**?

_____

49. Which word or words have a root meaning **heat**?

_____

laboratory

suspend

sonic

dormant

telephone

thermometer

depend

mobility

transfer

biography

visible

manual

dormitory

video

manufacture

ferry

Name _____ 16 _____

Fifth Grade Book of Language Tests

Read these meanings of the word *bitter*. Write the letter of the meaning that is used in each sentence below.

A. sour   C. painful
B. stinging, severe   D. angry, mean

____ 50. The race was a bitter disappointment.

____ 51. What a bitter argument this is!

____ 52. It's bitter cold outside.

____ 53. That lemonade is really bitter.

Read these meanings of the word *solid*. Write the letter of the meaning that is used in each sentence below.

A. unbroken   C. strong
B. firm or hard   D. reliable, dependable

____ 54. The house has a solid foundation.

____ 55. She's a solid member of the community.

____ 56. How solid is the ice?

____ 57. A solid line of skiers descends the hill.

IDIOMS

A. Hold your horses.
B. Do it on the double!
C. Drop me a line.
D. Keep a stiff upper lip.
E. Don't cut corners.
F. Face the music.
G. Go out on a limb.
H. Take the heat.

I. Stop horsing around.
J. Bite the bullet.
K. You're pulling my leg
L. You're ripping me off.
M. You spilled the beans.
N. Don't blow your top.
O. Don't skimp on money.
P. Make no bones about it.

Write the letter of the **idiom** that matches each definition.

____ 58. Stop fooling around.

____ 59. Get straight to the point.

____ 60. Hurry up.

____ 61. You're teasing me.

____ 62. Be patient.

____ 63. Accept the punishment that's coming.

____ 64. Don't get emotional.

____ 65. Take a chance.

____ 66. You gave away the secret.

____ 67. Write to me.

____ 68. Don't lose your temper.

____ 69. Don't be cheap or use poor materials.

____ 70. Accept the blame for something.

STOP

Name _____

17

LITERAL COMPREHENSION

Name _____

Possible Correct Answers: 40

Date _____

Your Correct Answers: _____

1. Fran has ridden 200 different roller coasters. There is nothing in the world she would rather do than ride a coaster. You could say she is a roller coaster fanatic! Her favorite coaster is *The Colossal Fire Dragon* in Farmington, Utah. She has ridden it 68 times.

What is the main idea of this paragraph?
   a. Fran travels all over the country.
   b. Fran lives in Utah.
   c. Fran loves riding roller coasters.
   d. Fran prefers *The Colossal Fire Dragon* because she has ridden it 68 times.

2. Ice climbing is possibly the most extreme sport of all. The extreme heights and extremely slippery surfaces make it terribly risky. In addition, sudden and unexpected weather conditions can change the conditions of the ice and cause danger for the climber. The best chances for safe climbing come to ice climbers that train well and plan carefully, use top quality equipment, pay serious attention to ice and weather conditions, and climb with skilled team members.

What is the main idea of this paragraph?
   a. Climbers can increase their chances of surviving the dangers of ice climbing.
   b. No one should climb an ice waterfall alone.
   c. Ice conditions can change suddenly, causing climbing to be dangerous.
   d. Ice climbing is dangerous and should be avoided.

3. Every July, the World Championship Bathtub Races are held on Vancouver Island in Canada. The world record holder for this sport did not set the record in this race, however. In 1987, Greg mutton moved his bathtub along a 36–mile course in 1 hour, 27 minutes, and 22 seconds. His race took place in Australia.

What is the main idea of this paragraph?
   a. The world record for bathtub racing was not set at the World Championship Bathtub Races.
   b. Bathtub races are held in Australia.
   c. 1½ hours is a fast time for a bathtub race.
   d. The world record for bathtub racing was set in Canada.

4.

A. Did you ever wonder how a hot air balloon gets up into the air? **B.** A hot air balloon rises because the hot air inside the balloon is lighter than the cooler, heavier air around it. **C.** The balloon needs lift to carry the weight of its and equipment. **D.** A propane torch is used to heat the air in the balloon until it is at least 100° hotter than the outside air temperature. **E.** Since the heated air is lighter than the air around it, the cooler air actually lifts the balloon and holds it up. **F.** The pilot can continue to make the balloon go up or stay level by reheating the air or letting some hot air escape.

Which sentence contains the main idea?
A   B   C   D   E   F

Fifth Grade Book of Language Tests

Copyright ©2000 by Incentive Publications, Inc., Nashville, TN.

1. An extreme sport called caving is not for everyone. 2. But some daring adventurers travel deep into the earth to explore regions that few people ever see. 3. Cavers take special equipment for their trips into deep caves. 4. Each explorer needs three or more reliable sources of light, a helmet, good boots and gloves, and special clothing. 5. On some trips, climbing equipment is needed. 6. If cavers plan to explore underground rivers or pools, they may carry scuba equipment or inflatable rafts.

7. Inside the caves, explorers face many dangers. 8. Some cavers get lost and are not able to find their way out. 9. Others die from falls, drowning, hypothermia, or shortage of oxygen. 10. Why do cavers get involved in this dangerous sport? 11. For many, it is challenging venture into places that are hidden from most visitors. 12. Others are hoping to find treasure. 13. Still others appreciate the beauty of the caves or enjoy the thrill of a dangerous adventure. 14. Whatever the reasons, the sport is more than just an adventure. 15. It is extremely risky business.

uh oh

5. Which sentences give details supporting the opinion that caving is dangerous? Write the sentence numbers.

_____

6. Which sentences give details describing special equipment used by cavers? Write the sentence numbers.

_____

7. Which is *not* one of the reasons given for taking part in this sport?

a. to win honors, medals, or prize money

b. to find treasure

c. for the challenge

d. for the thrill and danger

e. to see places most people never see

f. to enjoy the beauty of caves

Circle the letter of the best title for each article below.

The largest painting ever done by one artist is The Battle of Gettysburg. Paul Pilippoteaux finished it in 1883. It's about as big as a football field. No wonder it took over 2 years to paint!	The largest supply of sunken treasure in the world lies on the bottom of the Atlantic Ocean off the coast of the Bahamas. There are about 2000 Spanish galleons that sank in the 16th century.	The largest cake ever baked weighed 58 tons. It was baked to celebrate the 100th birthday of a town in Alabama. No information is available about how many people it took to eat the cake.

8.   a. Pilippoteaux's Paintings
     b. Painting on Football Fields
     c. The World's Largest Painting
     d. Battlefield Painting

9.   a. Valuable Sunken Treasure
     b. The Largest Treasure Stash
     c. Sunken Spanish Galleons
     d. Searching for Treasure

10.   a. What a Cake!
     b. A Birthday Celebration
     c. Who Ate the Cake?
     d. Alabama's 100th Birthday

Name _____

Fifth Grade Book of Language Tests

A.
The Sunday Mail Tribune
October 2, 1999
Climbers Reach Peak in 2 Weeks

B.
Portland Daily
January 2, 2000
Blizzard Hits Southern Oregon

C.
Evening Sun Times
July 7, 1999
SASQUATCH SITED IN OREGON

D.
The Daily Tidings
October 9, 1999
SCUBA DIVERS FIND LOST TREASURE

E.
The Town Gazette
July 4, 1996
Yacht Race In Its 30ᵗʰ Day

F.
The Morning News
May 15, 1998
High Wire Walker Performs at 1350 Feet

G.
The Cherrytown Herald
February 22, 1966
Oregonian Breaks Speed Skiing Record

11. Which events were reported in the same week? Write the letters of the headlines.

   _____

12. Which reported events happened in the same state? Write the letters.

   _____

13. What was broken on February 22, 1966?

   _____

14. Which event happened most recently?

   _____

15. On what date did the yacht race begin?

   _____

While the noble knight, Sir Frederick, was enjoying a vacation at a castle by the sea, he received news that a dreadful dragon was threatening his home village. In no time at all, Sir Frederick was facing the grandest dragon he had ever seen. Fearless Frederick wasted no time. He snarled at the dragon with such fierceness that the dragon turned and raced in the other direction, and was never seen again. Frederick never even had to use his sword.

16. In the passage above, which happened second?
   a. Sir Frederick faced the dragon.
   b. Sir Frederick snarled at the dragon.
   c. Frederick vacationed by the sea.
   d. Sir Frederick received bad news.

17. This limerick is out of order. Number the lines in the right order.

   _____ **Of the dragons so near,**

   _____ **It's just that his suit was too tight.**

   _____ **For months kept refusing to fight.**

   _____ **He didn't have fear**

   _____ **It's strange that Sir Guilford, the knight**

Name _____

Fifth Grade Book of Language Tests

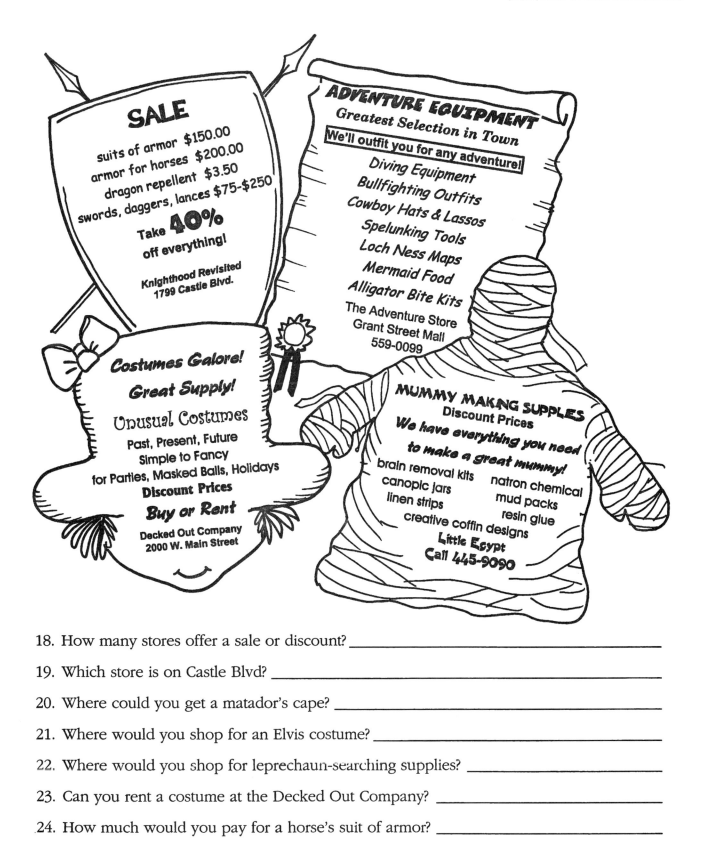

SALE

suits of armor $150.00
armor for horses $200.00
dragon repellent $3.50
swords, daggers, lances $75-$250

Take **40%** off everything!

Knighthood Revisited
1799 Castle Blvd.

ADVENTURE EQUIPMENT
Greatest Selection in Town

We'll outfit you for any adventure!

Diving Equipment
Bullfighting Outfits
Cowboy Hats & Lassos
Spelunking Tools
Loch Ness Maps
Mermaid Food
Alligator Bite Kits

The Adventure Store
Grant Street Mall
559-0099

Costumes Galore!
Great Supply!
Unusual Costumes

Past, Present, Future
Simple to Fancy
for Parties, Masked Balls, Holidays
Discount Prices
Buy or Rent

Decked Out Company
2000 W. Main Street

MUMMY MAKING SUPPLES
Discount Prices

We have everything you need
to make a great mummy!

brain removal kits
canopic jars
linen strips
creative coffin designs
natron chemical
mud packs
resin glue

Little Egypt
Call 445-9090

18. How many stores offer a sale or discount? _____

19. Which store is on Castle Blvd? _____

20. Where could you get a matador's cape? _____

21. Where would you shop for an Elvis costume? _____

22. Where would you shop for leprechaun-searching supplies? _____

23. Can you rent a costume at the Decked Out Company? _____

24. How much would you pay for a horse's suit of armor? _____

25. Which stores list phone numbers in their ads? _____

26. What it the chemical that's needed for preserving a mummy? _____

Name _____

Fifth Grade Book of Language Tests

Read the report and examine the diagram. Use both to answer the questions.

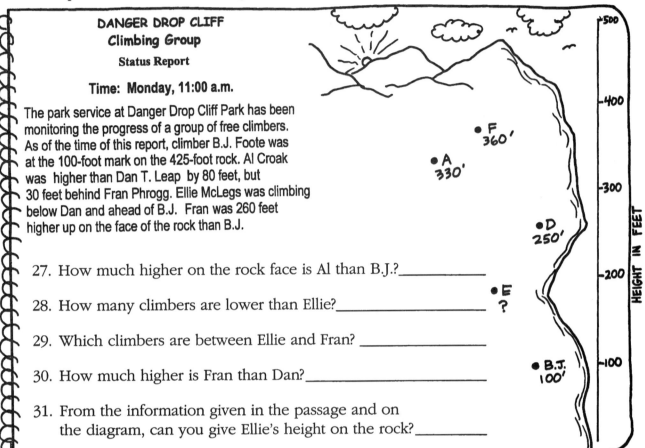

DANGER DROP CLIFF
Climbing Group
Status Report

Time: Monday, 11:00 a.m.

The park service at Danger Drop Cliff Park has been monitoring the progress of a group of free climbers. As of the time of this report, climber B.J. Foote was at the 100-foot mark on the 425-foot rock. Al Croak was higher than Dan T. Leap by 80 feet, but 30 feet behind Fran Phrogg. Ellie McLegs was climbing below Dan and ahead of B.J. Fran was 260 feet higher up on the face of the rock than B.J.

27. How much higher on the rock face is Al than B.J.?_____

28. How many climbers are lower than Ellie?_____

29. Which climbers are between Ellie and Fran? _____

30. How much higher is Fran than Dan?_____

31. From the information given in the passage and on the diagram, can you give Ellie's height on the rock?_____

32. Follow these directions carefully to complete the drawing in the box.

1) Connect A to B
2) Connect A to C
3) Connect B to D
4) Connect B to E
5) Connect C to L
6) Connect D to S
7) Connect Q to C
8) Connect U to D
9) Connect P to C
10) Connect D to W
11) Connect C to O
12) Connect N to C
13) Connect D to X
14) Connect T to D
15) Connect C to M
16) Connect D to V
17) Draw an arc from L to M to N to O to P to Q to L
18) Draw an arc from S to T to U to V to W to X to S

Copyright ©2000 by Incentive Publications, Inc., Nashville, TN.

THE THRILLING WORLD OF EXTREME SPORTS
Table of Contents

33. Which pages cover snowboarding? _____

34. Which sport covers the most pages? _____

35. How many kinds of diving are covered? _____

36. What pages give information about safety? _____

37. What pages cover sports that involve skiing? _____

38. Can you learn about sky surfing in Chapter II? _____

39. Which category of sports gets the most coverage? _____

40. In what two places could you probably find a definition of B.A.S.E. Jumping?

_____

_____

Name _____

Fifth Grade Book of Language Tests

INFERENTIAL & EVALUATIVE COMPREHENSION

Name _____

Possible Correct Answers: 35

Date _____

Your Correct Answers: _____

According to the 1999 *Guinness Book of Records*, the record for the longest paper clip chain is 16 miles, 978 yards long. Anyone wishing to challenge the current record must follow some rules for the paper clip chain category. The paper clips used must be no longer than 1½ inches, and each paper clip must hook into the end of another clip. No more than 60 people can work together to make a chain, and the chain must be created within a 24–hour time period.

1. The main idea of this passage is:
   a. A new paper clip chain record has been set.
   b. There are certain rules to follow in order to challenge the paper clip chain record.
   c. The *Guinness Book of Records* wants people to challenge their records.
   d. The longest paper clip chain ever made is 16 miles, 978 yards in length.

Al, a championship alligator wrestler, lives near the Everglades Swamp in south Florida. This year he spent only about thirteen weeks at home. The rest of the time, he traveled to Central America, Asia, Australia, and South America to wrestle gators. Searching for new swamps, new adventures, and new alligators, he travels more than he stays at home.

2. From this paragraph, you can tell:
   a. The author disapproves of Al's sport.
   b. The author envies Al.
   c. The author thinks this sport is foolish.
   d. none of these

3. From the passage, you can conclude: *(Circle all correct answers.)*
   a. Al does not like his home.
   b. Al has lived in south Florida for many years.
   c. Al is good at alligator wrestling.
   d. Al is away from home about three-fourths of the year.

4. The main idea of this passage is:
   a. Al has won many alligator wrestling contests.
   b. Al is not satisfied with the local alligators.
   c. Al has wrestled alligators in South and Central America.
   d. Al spends a lot of time traveling to pursue his interest in alligator wrestling.

24

April 15

Dear Frankie,

*   I should have known that you would grow up to be a frogman. You always loved hearing the stories about Grandpa Swamp and his escapades as a Navy Seal. But even so, I'm not ready for this news that you are working on your scuba license. Of course, I cannot forget what happened to your grandfather.*

*   Please, make sure that your training is very good. Remember everything they teach you. Take more than one class. Most scuba diving injuries and deaths are caused by human mistakes.*

*   There are so many dangers. Watch out for rocks and coral—these can cut your body or your equipment. Don't go nosing around barracudas or sharks. Always stay with your partner. And don't go into any underwater caves!*

*   You could be carried away from the boat or your partner by strong currents. You could descend too quickly and get brain damage! You could also get hypothermia and lose your senses. I hope you know that the pressure underwater can cause drowsiness, and that is very dangerous for a diver.*

*   Maybe you could find some other sport that would be less expensive. Have you tried soccer?*

Love,

Mom

5. The main point that the letter-writer makes is:
   - a. Scuba diving is dangerous.
   - b. The son's scuba class is not a good one.
   - c. Scuba diving can cause brain damage.
   - d. Grandpa Swamp was a skilled frogman.

6. What is the letter-writer's purpose?
   - a. to let her son know she supports his efforts to become a scuba diver
   - b. to warn her son of the dangers of diving
   - c. to make her son feel bad about what happened to Grandpa Swamp
   - d. to teach him about scuba diving

7. Based on the letter, which of these is most likely to be true?
   - a. The mother has some knowledge about scuba diving.
   - b. The mother is a scuba diver.
   - c. The mother knows nothing about the sport.

8. When mom suggests Frankie find a less expensive sport, what does she really mean?
   - a. She is upset about the cost of scuba diving.
   - b. She wants him to be a soccer player.
   - c. She worries that he will run out of money.
   - d. She wishes he had chosen a less dangerous sport.

9. From this letter, you can infer that:
   - a. Grandpa wanted Frankie to be a frogman.
   - b. Something terrible, related to scuba diving, happened to grandpa.
   - c. Mother has not seen Frankie for a long time.
   - d. None of these

Name _____

     Fifth Grade Book of Language Tests

Are You Ready?

If you ever plan to do any adventuring in space, you will need to know how astronauts get along on a space mission.

When you head into space, the ordinary environment of life is gone. There is no air, sunshine, day and night, or gravity. As soon as your shuttle takes off, your body will feel squished and squashed.

Fortunately, you'll have a space suit made of fifteen plastic layers that supplies you with oxygen and removes carbon dioxide and other waste products. The suit keeps the atmospheric pressure right for your body and also keeps you warm. It has a special drink bag and a camera for sending pictures to the cockpit.

Everything in the world of the astronaut is without gravity. Living without gravity is quite a bit different from your normal life! You will have to sleep, move, eat, and stay healthy in a place where everything floats around. At night, you will be tied to your bunk or sleep in a special sleeping suit. Your dinner would float away if it were not securely wrapped in a package.

Living without day and night is strange, too. Someone will have to tell you when it's time for you to sleep.

Sounds thrilling— doesn't it? Do you still want to head off into space?

10. The author's purpose is:
   a. to give information
   b. to defend the U.S. space program
   c. to warn you not to go to space
   d. to shock you with strange space facts

11. The main idea of this passage is:
   a. Space travel is dangerous.
   b. Astronauts need special equipment to deal with life in space.
   c. Space travel is great fun.
   d. Living without gravity is difficult.

Label each statement from the passage F (fact) or O (opinion).

_____ 12. When you head into space, the ordinary environment of life on earth is gone.

_____ 13. There is no sunshine, day or night, or gravity.

_____ 14. Living without gravity is quite a bit different from your normal life!

_____ 15. Sounds thrilling, doesn't it?

In each pair of sentences below, one sentence tells a cause. The other tells the effect. Mark each sentence C (cause) or E (effect).

_____ 16. Sixteen-inch footprints appeared in a meadow at the edge of a Washington forest.

_____ 17. A group of scientists and curious neighbors set off into the forest on a Bigfoot hunt.

_____ 18. The Cannonball coaster has been closed indefinitely.

_____ 19. There have been three accidents this year on Adventure Land's largest roller coaster.

Name _____

Fifth Grade Book of Language Tests

The current time is noon.

The last surfer to arrive has a green surfboard.

Darla has been surfing for 3 hours.

Fran and Al have been surfing for more than 5 hours.

The two surfers who arrived earliest are wearing wet suits.

The surfer with the red surfboard is not wearing a wet suit.

Carla has been surfing longer than Darla but less than Fran and Al.

From the information shown, can you infer that these statements are true? (Write yes or no.)

_____ 20. Al is wearing a wet suit.

_____ 21. Carla began surfing around 9:30 a.m.

_____ 22. Darla's surfboard is green.

_____ 23. Fran began surfing before 7:00 a.m.

Kris climbs buildings. He won't rest until he has conquered all the highest buildings in the city. Kris tries to get permission to climb each building. But if climbing is not allowed, he finds a way to do it anyway. A new skyscraper is being completed in the City Center Complex. Authorities have publicized the ban against climbing this building.

24. What do you think Kris will do?
   a. Try to get permission to climb the building, but climb it even if he cannot.
   b. Honor the ban against climbing the new skyscraper.
   c. Climb the building without asking for permission.
   d. Give up climbing altogether.

Yolanda has a video collection of world championship yacht races. She has purchased every one she can find. Now she is running out of the money to keep buying these tapes. Her friend Samantha has offered to let her borrow a collection of surfing tapes. Another friend, Fred, has a new TV satellite system and a subscription to all the news and sports channels. He has invited her to come and watch it any time.

25. What is Yolanda most likely to do now?
   a. She is likely to put aside her love of yachting and turn her attention to surfing.
   b. She is likely to sell some of her older yachting tapes to get money for buying new ones.
   c. She is likely to try to tape some yacht races from Fred's TV satellite system.
   d. She is not likely to do any of these.

Name _____

27

26. Based on the information given in the ads, which generalizations could you make?
    (Circle all that apply.)
    a. A snowboarder could shop any day of the week.
    b. Snowboard equipment could be rented at either shop.
    c. The Extreme Shop offers more services than Big Air Snowboards.
    d. Both shops have a large collection of snowboard supplies.
    e. A snowboarder is offered a wide range of times during which to shop.

27. What evidence can you gain from either ad to support the Extreme Shop's claim that it has
    the largest selection in town?
    a. The ads compare the sizes of the stores.
    b. The Extreme Shop ad shows that it carries more kinds of items.
    c. The ads describe the number of brands carried.
    d. Big Air Snowboards describes itself as a small store.
    e. There is no evidence.

Name _____

Six barefoot skiers took terrible falls during the ski show. Follow-up interviews revealed that all of these skiers had drunk orange juice for breakfast. Other skiers in the show had not had orange juice for breakfast. The interviewer concluded that the skiers' falls were caused by the orange juice.

28. Based on the information given in the article, why would this interviewer's conclusion be judged inaccurate?
    a. The other possible explanations for the falls were not discussed.
    b. The interviewer did not interview all the skiers in the show.
    c. It is not possible for orange juice to cause a skier to fall.
    d. The falls were probably caused by rough water.

Can the following conclusions reasonably be drawn from the information given on the chart? Write *yes* or *no* for each one.

GREAT DANCE RECORDS

KIND of RECORD	The Dance or Dancers	Date	Number or length
Largest Dance Occasion	Moonlight Serenade Dance Buffalo, NY	1984	25,000 people
Largest Single Dance (Everyone dancing at once)	Square Dance Louisville, KY	1983	20,000 dancers
Longest Dance Line	The Super Conga Dance Miami, FL	1988	119,986 dancers in a line
Longest Dancing Dragon	School children in Great Britain	1989	985 feet long
Most Exhausting Dance	Mike Ritof & Edith Boudreaux Chicago, IL	1930-1931	5,148 hours, 28 $\frac{1}{2}$ minutes
Lowest Height Limbo Stick Anyone Danced Under	Dennis Walston Kent, WA	1991	6 inches from floor

_____ 29. The setting for the Super Conga Dance was larger than the setting of the Moonlight Serenade Dance.

_____ 30. The longest dancing dragon was about the same length as the longest dance line.

_____ 31. More adults than children participate in dance contests.

_____ 32. Dancing 5,148 hours is harder than dancing under a 6–inch high limbo stick.

_____ 33. Dennis Walston has a very flexible body.

_____ 34. Dancing 5,148 hours is more tiring than dancing under a 6–inch high limbo stick.

_____ 35. Square dancing is more exhausting than other dances.

Name _____ 29 _____

Fifth Grade Book of Language Tests

LITERATURE SKILLS

Name _____

Possible Correct Answers: 55

Date _____

Your Correct Answers: _____

ONLY THE NIGHT KNOWS

Hiding in the deep shadows of the trees, the silent viewer watched the dark figure on the balcony. Slowly, stealthily, soundlessly, she crept across the balcony. Her tip-toe steps were soft as air. No one must hear her! The hush of the night was so huge, that any sound would be like crashing thunder splitting the air.

Oh, so smoothly, she reached the edge of the wide balcony. Tying the precious bundle to her long rope, she lowered it cautiously to the ground. With just as much care, she eased her body over the top of the balcony rail and slid down after the bundle. On the ground, she tied the bundle around her waist and vanished into the dark tangles of the vines and bushes.

Eyes followed her until the darkness swallowed her up. The quiet watcher made no attempt to follow her. Only the wide-eyed night knows who she was and where she was going.

1. The setting of the story is _____

_____

2. Who is the main character? _____

_____

3. Who is (are) the supporting character(s)?

_____

_____

4. What literary device is used in the title?
   a. hyperbole (exaggeration)
   b. alliteration
   c. personification
   d. repetition
   e. none of these

5. What is the genre (or form) of literature?
   a. essay
   b. article
   c. poem
   d. imaginary story
   e. myth
   f. tall tale
   g. report
   h. fable

6. This piece shows that the main character is:
   a. sinister
   b. a hero
   c. cautious
   d. reckless

7. Which is the best plot summary?

   a. A mysterious figure watched a burglar escape over a balcony with a bag of loot.

   b. As someone hid in the bushes to watch, a mysterious figure carrying a bundle climbed down from a balcony and disappeared into the night.

   c. On a dark night, a mysterious person climbed over a balcony and took a bundle of valuables away.

   d. A stranger witnessed a robbery in the night but did not follow the robber.

30

TERROR IN SCOTLAND

I've seen the fierce winged dragon
With mouth of flame and smoke,
And dreamed of the elusive Sasquatch
Still chasing me when I awoke.

I've ridden the great Greek Satyr
With body part man, part beast.
Done battle with the monstrous Hydra
Who wore nine heads, at least!

I've flown on the grotesque Griffin
Eagle head, lion body and tail.
Come face to face with a Yeti,
And shuddered till I grew pale.

I've danced with a mighty Unicorn
(Now does that sound absurd?)
Escaped from a deadly Siren,
A creature half woman, half bird.

But I've never shrieked in horror,
Never trembled and shook with dread.
I have never cried like a baby,
Nor stopped breathing like the dead.
No, I never knew sheer terror,
Not awake or asleep, I confess...
Until I saw, for a moment
The Monster of Loch Ness...
The massive
rising
grasping
writhing
SERPENT
of
Loch
Ness.

8. The form (genre) of this piece is:

   _____

9. The theme of the piece is:
   a. travel   c. adventure & danger
   b. flying   d. outlandish dreams

10. The mood of the last verse is:
    a. anger   c. silliness
    b. fear   d. worry

11. Write two phrases the writer uses to communicate her feeling of terror.

    _____

    _____

12. List five words the writer uses to strengthen the idea that each of the other creatures were terrible in their own right.

    _____

    _____

    _____

    _____

    _____

13. What words does the writer use to communicate the horrible nature of the Loch Ness monster?

_____

14. Does the statement below accurately summarize this piece of literature?   **yes   no**

   I've met several fierce creatures, but the Loch Ness Monster scared me the most.

Name _____

Fifth Grade Book of Language Tests

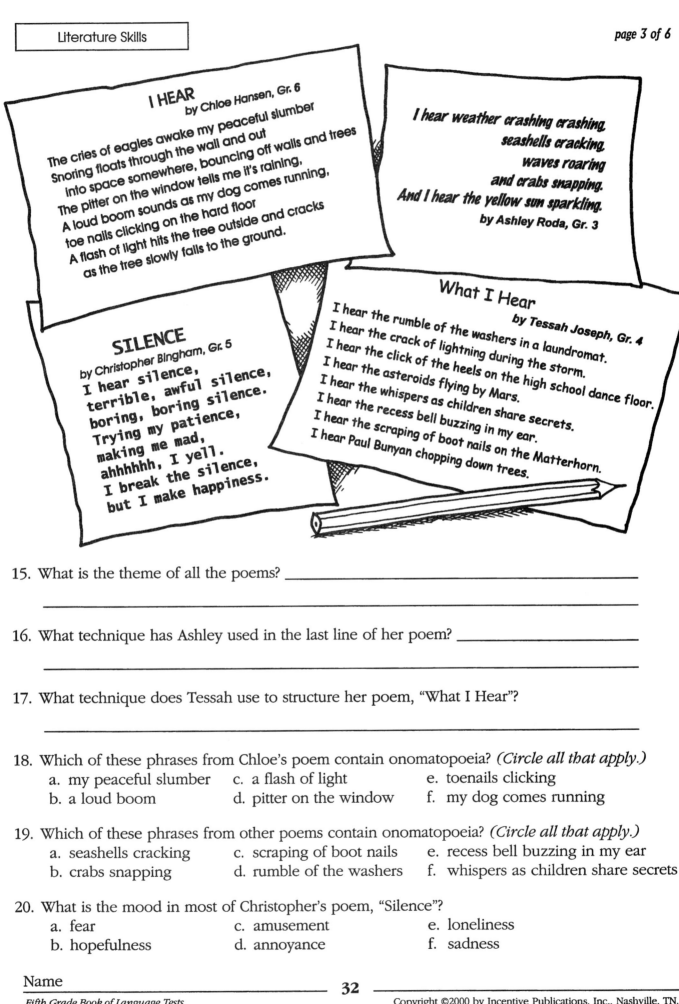

I HEAR
by Chloe Hansen, Gr. 6

The cries of eagles awake my peaceful slumber
Snoring floats through the wall and out
Into space somewhere, bouncing off walls and trees
The pitter on the window tells me it's raining,
A loud boom sounds as my dog comes running,
toe nails clicking on the hard floor
A flash of light hits the tree outside and cracks
as the tree slowly falls to the ground.

I hear weather crashing crashing,
seashells cracking,
waves roaring
and crabs snapping.
And I hear the yellow sun sparkling.
by Ashley Roda, Gr. 3

SILENCE
by Christopher Bingham, Gr. 5
I hear silence,
terrible, awful silence,
boring, boring silence.
Trying my patience,
making me mad,
ahhhhhh, I yell.
I break the silence,
but I make happiness.

What I Hear
by Tessah Joseph, Gr. 4
I hear the rumble of the washers in a laundromat.
I hear the crack of lightning during the storm.
I hear the click of the heels on the high school dance floor.
I hear the asteroids flying by Mars.
I hear the whispers as children share secrets.
I hear the recess bell buzzing in my ear.
I hear the scraping of boot nails on the Matterhorn.
I hear Paul Bunyan chopping down trees.

15. What is the theme of all the poems? _____

_____

16. What technique has Ashley used in the last line of her poem? _____

_____

17. What technique does Tessah use to structure her poem, "What I Hear"?

_____

18. Which of these phrases from Chloe's poem contain onomatopoeia? *(Circle all that apply.)*
    a. my peaceful slumber   c. a flash of light   e. toenails clicking
    b. a loud boom   d. pitter on the window   f. my dog comes running

19. Which of these phrases from other poems contain onomatopoeia? *(Circle all that apply.)*
    a. seashells cracking   c. scraping of boot nails   e. recess bell buzzing in my ear
    b. crabs snapping   d. rumble of the washers   f. whispers as children share secrets

20. What is the mood in most of Christopher's poem, "Silence"?
    a. fear   c. amusement   e. loneliness
    b. hopefulness   d. annoyance   f. sadness

Name _____

32

The lines and sentences below use
the literary devices shown on Fran's list.
Identify at least one device used for each example.
Write the code letter on the line beside the example.

A = alliteration
H = hyperbole
I = idiom
O = onomatopoeia
P = personification
PN = pun
S = simile
M = metaphor
R = rhyme
RT = rhythm
RP = repetition

_____21. **The queen is quite quick at quilting!**

_____22. *Not by the hair of your chinny, chin chin!*

_____23. **Not a chance, my son, not a chance!**

_____24. **That new librarian has a mind like a magnet.**

_____25. *It was so hot that the chickens laid scrambled eggs.*

_____26. **My calculator is like an annoying little brother.**

_____27. *I've asked you a million times to clean your room.*

_____28. **Her wild eyes were volcanoes of fire burning into my soul.**

_____29. The music called out across the room and invited me to dance.

_____30. **Doesn't that new policewoman have an arresting smile?**

_____31. Seven skilled skiers sliced swiftly through the slippery snow.

_____32. *You are driving me up a wall with your constant complaining.*

_____33. **Today the clouds are dragons breathing fires of stinging raindrops.**

_____34. *A sneaky fog stretched out its long, silvery fingers, reaching for me.*

_____35. Hiring the plumber, Seymour Pipes, would be a drain on our budget.

_____36. *Giving that speech in front of 500 people was like having all my teeth pulled.*

_____37. I'm sorry to refuse your offer of dinner, but potatoes just don't appeal to me.

_____38. **What a job to drive through that mushy, slushy, rushing rain-soaked traffic!**

_____39. *Our favorite teacher, named Mrs. McCool, just dismissed us all early from school.*

_____40. Grouchy thunderclouds groaned and complained at the heavy load they carried.

Name

33

Fifth Grade Book of Language Tests

41. Which of these literary devices are NOT used in the poem?
(Choose all that are not used.)
   a. personification   d. metaphor   f. rhyme
   b. simile   e. idiom   g. hyperbole
   c. alliteration

42. The poet compares the wind to many different things.

   How many? _____

43. How does the poet feel about the wind?
   a. He is afraid of the wind.
   b. He admires the wind's characteristics.
   c. He is curious about the wind.
   d. He thinks the wind is harmful.

The Wind
by Joseph Zoline-Black, Gr. 4

The wind is a crystal clear icy breeze.
It is a strong giant, a gentle child,
a furious volcano,
a steady moving thing.
   It has feelings like us,
   like a rushing person,
   like a curious child,
   like a patient waving person.
Sometimes it dies,
Sometimes it's alive—faster than you and me.
The wind shakes us, calms us, freezes us,
It's a dirty job
      but something has to do it.

The most daring adventure you could try,
More dangerous than surfing the sky,
A challenge so wild,
Unsafe for adult or a child—
Is eating lunch at Williamsville High.

Our principal, Mr. MacDude,
Just loves cafeteria food.
He eats six lunches (or more);
Keeps another in his drawer.
Any surprise about his chronic bad mood?

Don't take a bite or a munch
On a school cafeteria lunch.
Try congealed chicken supreme
Or the slimy orange carrots in cream,
And you will be sorry—a bunch!

If you're foolish enough to chance
A lunch at our school, West Side Manse,
You'll soon have to trade,
Your place in sixth grade
For a spot in the town's ambulance.

44. What common theme do the 4 poems above share?_____

45. Write a line which contains an image that affects your senses. _____

46. What was most likely the purpose the authors had in mind when they wrote these?
   a. to convince people not to eat school lunches
   b. to complain to the school about the lunch program
   c. to amuse their readers
   d. to inform someone about the contents of school lunches

47. The tone of these limericks is:
   a. playful   b. serious   c. argumentative   d. hostile

Each selection below is taken from a different form of literature.
Write the correct form below each selection. (Choose from the forms shown in the oval.)

King: What news do you have to report?

Sir Loin: The knights are weary, your highness.

King: Well, tell them that if they want to keep
their jobs, they should wake up! Get out there
and win this battle by midnight!

Sir Loin: Yes, your majesty.

48._____

Why was the little shoe crying?
Because his mama was a loafer
and his papa was a sneaker.

49._____

*It was after high school that I decided
to become a circus performer. Little
did I realize how much time it would
take to learn high wire walking! After
hundreds of falls, and four broken bones,
I began to lose my interest in this venture.*

50._____

"What? Someone has let all the bulls
loose?" shrieked the rodeo manager.
His assistant replied, "Well, all but one.
The old bull was too large to squeeze
through the opening." The manager
was frantic. "We have only two days,"
he moaned, "until the next show."

51._____

joke

essay

recipe

biography

autobiography

LETTER

dialogue

news report

advertisement

PLAY

POEM

Feel stronger in 10 days,
or your money will be
refunded in full.

53._____

The city zoo has purchased three
new elephants from Malaysia,
according to the zoo's press agent.
Officials plan to announce on
Sunday the details of the travel
arrangements for the animals.

54._____

Fold the maple syrup
gently into the whipped
egg whites. Drop spoonfuls
onto a greased pan.

55._____

Please see that the matter of the lost llamas
is cleared up immediately.

Yours truly,
Molly L. Ama

52._____

Writing Skills Checklists

Writing Test # 1:

WORD CHOICE & WORD USE

Test Location: pages 38–39

Skill	Test Items
Recognize and choose precise words for accurate meaning and interest	1–3
Recognize and choose effective words for strengthening written pieces	4–7
Recognize and choose active rather than inactive words and phrases	8–10
Identify words that help to create certain moods	11–13
Identify sentences which have words arranged in a manner that makes meaning clear	14–16
Identify words or phrases that are repetitive or unnecessary in a written passage	17–20
Recognize and choose words and phrases that produce strong visual images	21–25

Writing Test # 2:

FORMS & TECHNIQUES

Test Location: pages 40–43

Skill	Test Items
Recognize sensory appeal in passages; identify examples that appeal to particular senses	1–4
Recognize passages in which varied sentence structure and length makes the writing interesting and effective	5
Identify good use of details to support and enhance an idea	6
Identify examples and uses of expository, descriptive, persuasive, and imaginative writing	7–12
Recognize writing where form, style, or content fits a certain purpose for the writing	13–14
Recognize writing where form, style, or content appeals to a specific audience	15–16
Distinguish among different literary devices used to make writing effective	17–28
Identify examples and uses of exaggeration (hyperbole)	17
Identify examples and uses of personification	18, 22, 26
Identify examples and uses of sound devices such as alliteration and rhyme	19, 25
Identify uses of similes and metaphors	20, 21, 23, 24, 28
Identify examples and uses of idioms and puns	27
Distinguish among different writing forms; identify characteristics of different forms	29–35

Fifth Grade Book of Language Tests

Writing Test # 3:

CONTENT & ORGANIZATION

Test Location: pages 44–47

Skill	*Test Items*
Choose and use effective words in writing tasks	Task # 1
Create sentences that are clear and interesting	Task # 2
Put sentences in sensible sequence that makes meaning clear	Task # 3
Write clear questions to gain information	Task # 4
Create strong titles for written pieces	Task # 5
Create strong, attention-getting beginnings	Task # 6
Create strong, effective endings or conclusions	Task # 7
Include a clear main idea in a written passage	Task # 8
Show completeness and clear organization in a written piece	Task # 9
Use relevant details and examples to support a main idea	Task # 10

Writing Test # 4:

EDITING

Test Location: pages 48–51

Skill	*Test Items*
Recognize and replace overused, ordinary, or inactive words and phrases	Task # 1
Revise sentences for clarity	Task # 2
Eliminate excess or repetitive words or ideas in sentences	Tasks # 3 and # 10
Eliminate repetitive or unrelated ideas in passages	Tasks # 4 and # 10
Arrange ideas or sentences in proper sequence	Task # 5
Improve weak beginnings	Task # 6
Improve weak endings or conclusions	Task # 7
Replace weak or imprecise titles	Task # 8
Strengthen a passage by adding dialogue or changing existing text to dialogue	Task # 9
Revise writing for accuracy in punctuation, capitalization, and other conventions	Task # 10

Writing Test # 5:

WRITING PROCESS

Test Location: pages 52–59

Skill	*Test Items*
The writing process test is a test of writing performance. A scoring guide (pages 130–131) is used to enable the adult to give student writers a score of 1–5 in the areas of Content, Word Choice, Sentence Fluency, Organization, Voice, and Conventions.	Entire Test

---

37

WORD CHOICE & WORD USE

Name _____

Possible Correct Answers: 25

Date _____

Your Correct Answers: _____

Choose the most precise word for each blank.

1. Wild Harry took a _____ ride over Niagara Falls in a barrel.
   - a. interesting
   - b. perilous
   - c. nervous
   - d. fast
   - e. eventful
   - f. strange

2. Jana's best friend was _____ by her sudden and mysterious disappearance.
   - a. amused
   - b. troubled
   - c. interested
   - d. curious

3. The elephant _____ along heavily in the parade.
   - a. pranced
   - b. slid
   - c. walked
   - d. skipped
   - e. lumbered
   - f. wandered

Choose the word that is most effective for each blank.

4. The sunset threw a _____ orange glow across the rippling lake.
   - a. glamorous
   - b. nice
   - c. cute
   - d. spectacular
   - e. fancy
   - f. appetizing

5. Someone or something is _____ in the dark shadows, staring out at me with piercing eyes.
   - a. hiding
   - b. standing
   - c. lurking
   - d. playing

6. Enjoy a juicy broiled hamburger _____ with your favorite sauce.
   - a. covered
   - b. drenched
   - c. complete
   - d. topped

7. Oh, how we _____ as we hurried by the dark, creepy house!
   - a. shuddered
   - b. giggled
   - c. worried
   - d. sighed
   - e. whispered
   - f. shrugged

8. Which example shows active voice?
   - a. The peppers on my sandwich were spicy.
   - b. The spicy peppers bit my tongue.
   - c. Pickle juice was spicy on my tongue.

9. Circle the letters of the sentences that have an active verb.
   - a. A tornado tore through the town.
   - b. The tidal wave is a few miles off the coast.
   - c. Doesn't that black cloud look ominous?
   - d. Hurricane Alfred devastated the coastline.

10. Which sentences have an active verb?

    A. It appeared that the crime was a robbery.

    B. Broken glass covered the crime scene.

    C. Investigators examined every clue.

    D. The mystery became more puzzling.

    E. An idea sprang into the detective's mind!

    F. She shouted, "I know what happened!"

11. What mood would these words help to set?

hurry	*scurry*	*fast*
zip	*bustle*	*quick*
dart	*dash*	*race*

Write a word or a phrase to describe the mood.

_____

12. What mood would these words help to set?

giggled   *gleeful*   *chuckle*

lightheartedness

amusement   *delight*   *teasing*

Write a word or a phrase describing the mood.

_____

13. What mood would these words help to set?

puzzling   *hidden*   *secretive*

unknown   *invisible*

giggled   *gleeful*   *chuckle*

_____

14. Which sentence is written most clearly?
   a. Riding a fast horse, the wind picked up.
   b. The wind picked up while riding a fast horse.
   c. While I was riding a fast horse, the wind picked up.

15. Which sentence is written most clearly?
   a. Some students were scolded after throwing rocks by the principal.
   b. After throwing rocks, some students were scolded by the principal.
   c. After throwing rocks, the principal scolded some students.

16. Which sentence is written most clearly?
   a. At the circus, ice cream with sprinkles was given to the children.
   b. Ice cream was given to the children with sprinkles at the circus.
   c. Children were given ice cream at the circus with sprinkles.

Which sentences contain words or ideas that are repetitive or unnecessary?
(Circle the numbers.)

17. *The fake whipped cream in those cream puffs is not real.*

18. *You are not to climb that water tower, never!*

19. *Is it true that the bakery is missing all its doughnuts?*

20. *Yes! It is one hundred percent, totally true!*

Which sentences create strong visual images? *(Circle the numbers.)*

21. The moon is not shining tonight.

22. Last night's moon shimmered like a slice of silver ribbon in a black sky.

23. The cracking and popping sound of her gum hurt my ears.

24. Dripping red juices slowly slide across the road from the wrecked tomato truck.

25. Fluffy, sugary golden meringue tops the thick, yellow lemon cream of the pie.

Name

Fifth Grade Book of Language Tests

FORMS & TECHNIQUES

Name _____   Possible Correct Answers: 35

Date _____   Your Correct Answers: _____

Write the sense that is appealed to most strongly by each example.

Sensory Appeal

WHICH SENSE?
smell
hearing
taste
sight
touch or feeling

_____ 1. In the street outside Mac's Grill, the air is heavy with a greasy, oniony mist that makes me feel even more sick.

_____ 2. My heart pounds wildly in my chest as I wait for the ambulance.

_____ 3. The scream of the red sirens splits through the black night.

_____ 4. The flashing ambulance lights make my eyes squeeze shut.

5. Read the two versions of the story below. One version uses different sentence structure and sentence lengths throughout the story to make the writing more interesting. Which one has the most effective writing? *(Circle A or B.)*

A. The kids meant no harm. It was an ordinary evening and the four of them were just hanging around together. Well, in all honesty, maybe they were hoping for a little excitement. They ended up getting more excitement than a little. At first, it seemed like a good idea to spread out along the railroad tracks, lying down to listen for trains. "Was it true that you could hear the rumble of the tracks long before the sound of the whistle reached your ears?" they wondered. Joe found out that it was true. By the time he awoke to hear the rumble, however, his friends had fallen asleep in spots far away from him. They didn't answer when he shouted. It was too dark to see anyone. What could he do? The quiet adventure quickly turned into a nightmare as he ran along the tracks screaming their names. Then he heard the whistle.

B. It was an ordinary evening. The four friends were just hanging around together. They were hoping for a little excitement. They ended up getting a lot of excitement. They decided to lie down on the railroad tracks. They wanted to listen for trains. It seemed like a good idea. They wondered if they could hear the rumble on the tracks before they heard the whistle. Joe found out that he could. He heard the rumble. His friends were asleep far away from him. He shouted to them. They did not answer him. Where were they? It was too dark. What could he do? He ran along the track, screaming their names. The adventure turned into a nightmare. Then he heard the whistle of the train.

6. Read the following passage about a court case. Look for details in the writing that will be useful to the judge as he tries to understand the evidence. Circle these details.

SMALL CLAIMS COURT

Oliver brought a lawsuit against his former friend, Grady. The case was assigned to Judge Len Court. Both parties looked mad. Both of them were wearing suits. Oliver was asked to speak first. "Grady ate parts of all my best chocolate truffles," Oliver told the judge. "On Sunday evening, Grady came to my house. I showed him my box of truffles," Oliver explained. Oliver stopped to cough. "While he was in my room, I got a phone call and went downstairs," Oliver continued. "The next morning, I found that every truffle had a hole in it. Someone had eaten the middle of each one!" shouted Oliver. The judge asked why he was so sure it was Grady who ruined the truffles. Oliver explained that Grady had been the only one in his room all evening.

"Thank you, Oliver," said the judge. Grady was eager to have his turn. The judge turned to him and asked, "Did you eat the truffles?" Grady turned to face the judge. "No, your honor." Judge Court asked Grady what evidence he could give to prove that he was not the culprit. "I have one piece of evidence, sir." Grady scratched his head. "What is that?" the judge asked. "I am deathly allergic to chocolate," Grady stated simply.

For each piece of writing described, tell whether it is expository (EX), imaginative (IM), descriptive (D), or persuasive (P) writing. Write the code (EX, IM, D, or P) for each one.

_____ 7. an advertisement for baseball shoes

_____ 8. directions for building a kite

_____ 9. a tall tale about a boy would could ride tornadoes

_____ 10. an essay explaining someone's viewpoint about schools using the Internet for teaching

_____ 11. a science fiction story about a group of kids who travel through time to the 23rd century

_____ 12. a poster encouraging you to try the new lemon liver yogurt

Don't ever put watermelon seeds
In your mouth or in your ears,
Or you will have a watermelon patch
Covering your head in a few years.

Your skull will turn green
And form stripes like a rind
And sweet, pink juice
Will drip from your mind.

13. What is the purpose of the piece above?

a. to inform about a danger

b. to amuse the reader

c. to instruct about growing watermelon

d. to complain about kids playing with watermelon seeds

Name _____

41

14. The passage on the right is probably taken from a piece of writing whose purpose is to:

    a. convince someone to try a product
    b. explain the reason why something works
    c. give directions for putting something together
    d. describe a product

> 3. Match notch A to Notch B.
> 4. Place glue along the edges P.
> 5. Press Parts 1 and 2 together.
> 6. Hold 3 minutes.
> 7. Match Tab D to Tab E
> 8. Match Tab F to Tab G.
> 9. Nail Corner 4 to Corner 6.

Read these two pieces of writing. For each one, tell what audience the writer had in mind.

Health Watch

A serious bacterial infection is spreading through the state. A growing number of cases have been reported in the past week. Children are affected with the most serious symptoms of high fever and brain damage. The infection spreads by contact, with the most common source being dirt or soil from the ground. Caution your children and students to wash hands frequently and keep fingernails clean. Keep dirty hands away from their mouths.

If you play in the dirt, you'll get germs real quick!

If you eat with dirt on your hands, You'll wind up sick!

15. Audience: _____

16. Audience: _____

Write the letter of the literary device that matches each sentence below.
(A device may be used more than once.)

____ 17. It was so cold that my words froze before they reached your ears.

____ 18. The raging river gobbles up boats and swallows them whole.

____ 19. A little old lady from Dover has just found a seven-leaf clover.

____ 20. Little twin brothers are like double hurricanes.

____ 21. This homework is going as slowly as an opera.

____ 22. I'm sure that doughnut is calling to me!

____ 23. Life is a puzzle with pieces missing.

____ 24. My dad's meat loaf tastes like sawdust.

____ 25. Blotchy black blobs bubbled in the broth.

____ 26. The tea kettle hisses at me.

____ 27. I went out on a limb to get you that CD.

____ 28. Math is as slippery as wet spaghetti.

> *alliteration (A)*
>
> *exaggeration (E)*
>
> *idiom (I)*
>
> *metaphor (M)*
>
> *personification (P)*
>
> *rhyme (R)*
>
> *simile (S)*

Name _____

Fifth Grade Book of Language Tests

Each example shown on this page is part of a larger piece of writing. Read each example, then decide which of the kinds of writing listed below was the source. Write the source on the line.

speech	menu	letter	poem	biography
autobiography	essay	story	play	news article
advertisement	joke	diary	sermon	news editorial

What grit! What gall
To face a cavern deep.
What kind of nerves
To even dare such a plan?
What drives a heart
To place its fate
In a wire so thin?

29. _____

What did the canyon say to Sam McReevil?
What?
Drop in and see me any time!

30. _____

Tomorrow morning, Sam McReevil, age 28, of Bonnsville, will attempt the unthinkable. At 10:00 a.m. Mountain Standard Time, he will attempt to ride a motorcycle across the Grand Canyon on a 4 inch steel cable. According to his press agent, Bartholomew Green, Mr. McReevil has been preparing for two years for this stunt.

31. _____

Sam McReevil's boyhood was anything but ordinary. His mom admits that he had nine broken bones before he turned nine. He spent hours every day jumping off the barn into piles of hay, or climbing over electric fences.

32. _____

See the DARING McREEVIL
cross the
GRAND CANYON
Saturday, 10 a.m.
Bring your camera!
Bring your binoculars!

Follow the yellow signs to the gate.
Admission $5.00 adults $2.00 children

33. _____

High wire stunts are foolish and dangerous. The public lands should not be used for such nonsense. City officials and news reporters have more important things to do than chase after publicity hungry goofballs like this Sam McReevil.

34. _____

I thank you all for coming to witness this event. You have probably never seen anything like it. It is with great pride that I undertake this daring venture. I will not disappoint you.

35. _____

Name _____

43

CONTENT & ORGANIZATION

Name _____   Possible Correct Answers: 50

Date _____   Your Correct Answers: _____

This test is made up of 10 writing tasks. Your teacher will read your writing for each task, and will give a score of 1 to 5 points, depending on how completely you followed the directions.

TASK # 1

WORD USE: Think about your favorite food. Describe its wonderful characteristics for a restaurant menu. Think about the looks, smells, tastes, textures, and sounds of the food. Also think about how you feel when you eat and enjoy the food. Then write your description in a short paragraph in which every word is important. Try to use words that are precise, interesting, colorful, and unique. Give a title or name to this menu entry.

_____

_____

_____

_____

_____

_____

TASK # 2

CLEAR SENTENCES: Choose two of the following topics. For each one, write a clear interesting sentence that has something to do with the topic. The sentences can be any structure.

- a big disappointment   • a memory   • a wild storm
- a tough test   • an argument   • a wish
- something you'd like to forget   • a surprise   • a dream

1. _____

_____

2. _____

_____

TASK # 3

SENSIBLE SEQUENCE: These sentences make a clear story when they are placed in a sensible sequence. Number them (1 to 7) in an order that makes sense.

____ When it was over, we found our car in the neighbor's swimming pool.

____ Our car was hurled across the street like a plastic toy.

____ The tornado struck at dawn.

____ Suddenly the roar stopped and everything was still.

____ Slowly, we crept out of the shelter.

____ We hurried into the shelter.

____ A whirling black funnel headed straight for our house.

- someone who has been locked in a refrigerator for 8 hours

- a gorilla tamer who has just met a new, wild gorilla

- a Supreme Court Justice

- a championship sky-surfer

- a kid who has raced 3000 miles on a lawnmower

- someone who has ridden a rollercoaster for 14 days straight

- _____
  (your choice: Write it here.)

TASK # 4

CLEAR QUESTIONS: Choose one of the people described. Assume that you want to gain information about their work, predicament, or accomplishment. Write two good questions to ask the person that would help you get that information.

1. _____

   _____

   _____

2. _____

   _____

   _____

TASK # 5

STRONG TITLES: Write a good title or headline for each article or story. Make sure the title (or headline) is clearly a good label for the main idea of the written piece.

A man was found wandering on Main Street last night wearing tattered socks and no shoes. He was also missing his shirt, hat, glasses, the left leg of his pants, and his memory. He did not remember anything after seeing an approaching tornado. Police are searching for his family. Anyone having any information about his identity should call the city police at 555–2222.

I have always wondered why mom and dad got such a good deal when they bought this house. The day we moved in, I discovered the reason. My brother and I followed our parents up the broken, creaking stairs. We walked across a porch filled with cobwebs and then went in through a heavy, black door. We found ourselves standing in a hall as dark and damp as the inside of a whale.

Name _____

Fifth Grade Book of Language Tests

TASK # 6

STRONG BEGINNINGS: Write a strong beginning for one of these topics.
Make sure your beginning will grab the attention of the reader so well that
he or she will want to finish the entire piece of writing.

- learning to tame a lion
- a strange disappearance
- a visit with Bigfoot
- a dog who can read
- lizards who can dance
- a shocking letter
- an accident
- a terrible flood
- a disturbing discovery

_____

_____

_____

TASK # 7

STRONG ENDINGS: Write a strong ending for one of these topics.
Make your ending memorable. That means: after reading the ending, it will stay with the reader
because it is so effective, fresh, unusual, surprising, or shocking.

- an earthquake
- a wild sports event
- a mystery
- a person to avoid
- a person to meet
- a case of green earlobes
- an embarrassing moment
- a trip that didn't go well
- an unusual homework assignment

_____

_____

_____

TASK # 8

CLEAR MAIN IDEA: Write a short
letter expressing an opinion about
something in your town, your
school, your state, or your country.
Make sure that your letter contains a
main point or idea that is clearly
written. You might write about :

- someone you think
  deserves appreciation
- something that bothers you
- something you strongly support
- something that
  should be changed
- something you wish
  could happen
- something that is
  not working well

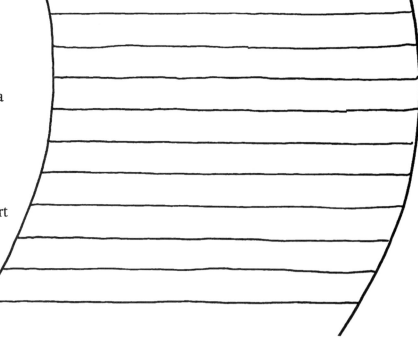

Name _____

47

TASK # 9

CLEAR ORGANIZATION: Write a description, story, or tall tale to go along with this picture. Make sure your writing has:

- A good title
- A strong beginning
- A strong middle
- A strong ending
- Details to explain the main idea

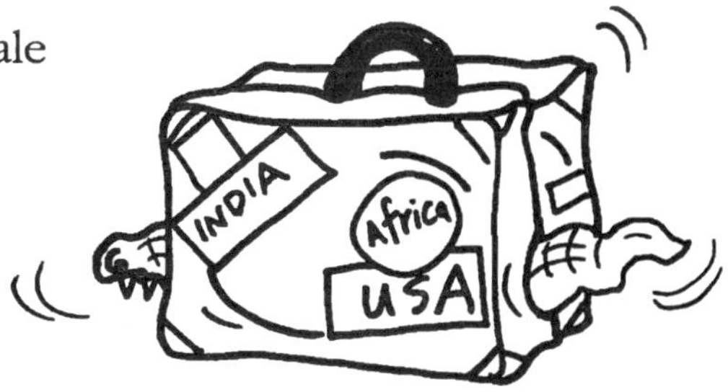

_____

_____
_____
_____
_____
_____
_____
_____
_____

TASK # 10

GOOD DETAILS: Fill in the blank to finish the opening sentence of the essay below. Then finish a paragraph that contains at least four details to support your first sentence. The details should make it clear to your reader why you would NOT want to visit this place. Give the essay a title.

_____

_____ is a place I would rather not visit—not ever!

_____
_____
_____
_____
_____
_____
_____
_____

Name _____

Fifth Grade Book of Language Tests

EDITING

Name _____

Date _____

Possible Correct Answers: 50

Your Correct Answers: _____

This test is made up of 10 editing tasks. Your teacher will read your writing on each one, and will give a score of 1 to 5 points, depending on how accurately you follow the directions for each task.

It was a <u>bad</u> idea to ride the rollercoaster when I was feeling <u>sick</u>. The Triple Loop looked <u>scary</u>. Once I got on, my stomach <u>hurt</u> as the rollercoaster <u>moved</u> up and down and <u>went</u> from side to side. I have never felt so <u>awful</u>!

EDITING TASK #1

IMPROVE WORD USE

1. Replace each ordinary word in the passage at left with a more colorful or interesting word. Write the new word or phrase above each underlined word.

2. Rewrite each sentence below to make it more active.

   a. The parade went on for four miles.

   _____

   _____

   b. Did you really have six eclairs for lunch?

   _____

   _____

EDITING TASK #2

CLARIFY SENTENCES: Re-write the following sentences to make the meaning clear.

1. Sitting on the top shelf of the closet, I found an old sandwich.

   _____

   _____

2. We heard about the robber who was caught on the radio.

   _____

   _____

3. I set the hot chocolate down beside my book that was too hot to handle.

   _____

   _____

Fifth Grade Book of Language Tests
Copyright ©2000 by Incentive Publications, Inc., Nashville, TN.

EDITING TASK #3
ELIMINATE EXCESS WORDS
Cross out the words that are repetitive or otherwise not needed.

1. In my opinion, I think that snowboards are not at all dangerous, even a bit.

2. She totally ate the whole pizza.

3. Jason drew seven three-sided triangles in his geometry design.

4. In addition, the sundae had marshmallow and whipped cream as well.

EDITING TASK #4
ELIMINATE UNRELATED IDEAS
Read each passage. Cross out any phrases, sentences, or ideas that are not related to the topic.

Officer! Officer! Come quickly! There are loud noises and screams around the corner outside a restaurant. I am an out-of-town visitor from Memphis. You must hurry. I heard breaking glass and I smelled smoke. The restaurant advertises on TV. There might be a fire. Follow me, I'll show you where it is. By the way, my name is Joe.

It is a terrible shame that the people of this city are not willing to support a new library. A city is poor without a good library. Kids and adults need the richness that comes from learning. Libraries supply all kinds of exciting information in many forms. Maybe if we had a good library, the police budget could be smaller, because people would be reading instead of causing trouble. A few more restaurants would be a good idea, too. And the town needs a better park.

EDITING TASK #5
IMPROVE SEQUENCE: These limericks do not make sense, because the ideas are not in a sensible sequence. Number the lines in each limerick so that the sequence creates a poem that makes sense.

___Keeps another in his drawer.

___Just loves cafeteria food.

___He eats six lunches (or more);

___No wonder he's in a chronic bad mood!

___Our principal, Mr. MacDude,

___You'll soon have to trade,

___For a spot in the town's ambulance.

___If you're foolish enough to chance

___Your place in sixth grade

___A lunch at our school, West Side Manse,

Name _____

Fifth Grade Book of Language Tests

EDITING TASK #6
STRENGTHEN BEGINNINGS
Revise each of these beginnings to make them stronger and more attention-getting for a reader.

1. It began at eight o'clock in the morning.

_____

2. This story is about something unusual.

_____

3. I want to convince you to try my favorite food.

_____

EDITING TASK #7
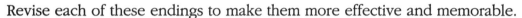
STRENGTHEN ENDINGS
Revise each of these endings to make them more effective and memorable.

1. And that is my warning about rock climbing alone.

_____

2. So ends the story of the mysterious disappearance of the tacos.

_____

3. Now, wasn't that funny?

_____

EDITING TASK #8
STRENGTHEN TITLES
Replace each title with one that is more accurate and more interesting.

_____
(New Title)
BUY CHOCOLATE CHIPS

If you want to get rid of acne, follow this advice for a guaranteed cure. Make a mixture of cream cheese and chopped deviled ham. Spread it on your face and rest for twenty minutes. Rinse it off with prune juice. If you are still having trouble after three days of this treatment, Use small dabs of cream cheese to stick a chocolate chip to each blemish on your face. Then, it won't matter if you have acne, because no one will be able to see it.

_____
(New Title)
HOW TO PAY TAXES

Something needs to be done about the tax structure in America. No family who has barely enough to pay for rent and food should have to pay 10% or 15% of that small amount. Poor people are too burdened by taxes. Also, there are too many loopholes for wealthier people. For everyone, the system is just too complicated. The government must work to simplify the forms and the rules. How can anyone understand them.

Name _____

EDITING TASK #9
ADD DIALOGUE

Rewrite the conversation from the cartoon below. Write it in a paragraph that includes dialogue. Use correct punctuation for the dialogue.

_____

_____

_____

_____

EDITING TASK #10
CORRECT CONVENTIONS

Fix the spelling, punctuation, capitalization, and grammar in this letter. Also, eliminate excess words or phrases. Cross out the errors and write the corrections above each line.

May 15, 1999

Dear editor

In my opinion, the new minature golf corse which the city has built owned by

the city should change its rules. It does not make sens to refuse kids under 18

to come unless they are with adults I thought the city bilt this corse to atract

kids and give them something good to do in the evenings. This is a wunderful

activity for kid. it is good for kids, but you are keeping them away. Most

teenagers want to go out for an activity with there friends, not there parents

Whose bad idea was this. I protest I hope this rule will be changed soon

Sincerely,
Amanda McLeggs

Fifth Grade Book of Language Tests

WRITING PROCESS

Name _____

Date _____

Possible Correct Answers: 30

Your Correct Answers: _____

The purpose of this test is to find out how well you can use the writing process to create a piece of written prose. The next page gives you ideas for writing and directions for doing the test. This page gives you some guidelines for writing a good paper.

Your writing will be scored on these six traits.
You can receive 1 to 5 points on each trait.
A good piece of writing scores at least 3 points in each trait.

TRAITS

CONTENT:

The writing is clear, interesting, and fun to read. The reader can easily understand the main point of the paper. You have used many details that grab the attention of the reader. You give information about your topic and clearly show what is happening.

WORD CHOICE:

The words are fresh and interesting. You have avoided overused, ordinary words. Your paper uses active verbs. You have used words and phrases that your reader will remember. The words strengthen your ideas and give them a good flavor.

VOICE:

The paper has your personal mark on it. It shows the feelings and personality of the writer. The reader can tell a human being wrote this paper. It talks directly to the reader and shows what you really think.

ORGANIZATION:

The paper starts with a catchy beginning. The writing builds to the important point, with plenty of connected details in a clear order. A reader will want to keep reading your paper. You avoid using a lot of unrelated ideas. Your paper has a good, memorable ending.

SENTENCES:

The sentences are clear and sound interesting. The sentences are different in length and structure. Your sentences do not all begin the same way. If you read your paper aloud, the sentences flow nicely together and sound smooth.

CONVENTIONS:

You have used punctuation and capitalization in the right places. Your spelling and grammar are correct. Each new idea is placed in a new paragraph.

Fifth Grade Book of Language Tests

DIRECTIONS
1) Choose ONE of the writing tasks (topics).
2) Use the space on page 3 to gather ideas about your topic.
3) Use page 3 to organize your ideas
4) Use pages 4 and 5 to write a rough draft.
5) Use the *Editor's Guide* on page 6 to help you polish your writing .
6) Use pages 7 and 8 for your final draft.

WRITING TASKS (Choose One)

TASK # 1   Three kids had an unusual adventure on their way home from school. **Make up a story** about what happened. Include the words, *"If they knew then what they know now, the three friends never would have taken that shortcut."*

TASK # 2   Think of a real or make-believe food *(such as tuna-fish artichoke ice cream)*. Describe it well and **convince** your reader that it is something to try.

TASK # 3   **Describe** a character that you would like to meet. Explain what makes this character so interesting to you. The character may be real or imaginary.

TASK # 4   **Tell a true story** about your most embarrassing experience or about any other experience you would rather not have again.

TASK # 5   Think about something you know how to do that others may not be able to do. (This can be something you can play, make, create, perform, or accomplish.) **Explain** how to do it.

Name _____

Fifth Grade Book of Language Tests

COLLECT IDEAS

Write down words, phrases, sentences, and ideas that you might want to include in your paper. Put down everything that comes to mind! You might not use it all, but keep brainstorming. Think of fresh and unusual ideas. Collect colorful words. Use another piece of paper if you need more space.

ORGANIZE IDEAS

Make an outline, web, or list to organize your ideas. Decide on a main idea for each paragraph. Pull together the ideas that support that idea.

Name

54

Use your outline or web from page 3 of this test to write a rough draft here.

ROUGH DRAFT

_____

(Title)

_____

_____

_____

_____

_____

_____

_____

_____

_____

_____

_____

_____

Name _____

Fifth Grade Book of Language Tests

ROUGH DRAFT, continued...

EDITOR'S GUIDE

CONTENT
___Does it make a clear main point that is easy to understand?
___Did I include examples or details that support the main point?
___Did I leave out details that don't relate to the main point?
___Does the paper show that I know something about the topic?
___Does it include fresh, interesting ideas?

ORGANIZATION
___Does it have a strong beginning that catches the reader's attention?
___Are the ideas written in an order that makes sense?
___Are the ideas that belong together grouped in the same paragraph?
___Will the reader want to keep on reading?
___Does the paper have a great, unusual ending?

WORD CHOICE
___Did I choose words that will capture the reader's imagination?
___Have I used some fresh, unusual, and colorful words or phrases?
___Have I used active verbs?
___Have I used words that make the meaning of the paper clear?

SENTENCES
___When I read the paper out loud, does it sound smooth?
___Are the sentences clear and interesting?
___Have I used different lengths of sentences?
___Have I used sentences that have different beginnings or structures?

VOICE
___Does my paper show personality?
___Does the writing show what I feel and think?
___Does the paper talk directly to the reader?

CONVENTIONS
___Have I used correct capitalization on sentences and names?
___Is my punctuation correct?
___Is my spelling correct?
___Have I used grammar correctly?
___Do all my paragraphs contain sentences on the same idea?
___Are all my paragraphs indented?

Name

57

FINAL DRAFT

_____

(Title)

_____

_____

_____

_____

_____

_____

_____

_____

_____

_____

_____

_____

_____

_____

_____

Name _____

Fifth Grade Book of Language Tests

FINAL DRAFT, continued...

_____

_____

_____

_____

_____

_____

_____

_____

_____

_____

_____

_____

_____

_____

_____

_____

_____

_____

_____

Name

Grammar & Usage Skills Checklists

Grammar & Usage Test # 1:

PARTS OF SPEECH

Test Location: pages 62–65

Skill	Test Items
Identify and distinguish among different parts of speech	1–17, 71–80
Recognize how a word is used in a sentence	13–17, 71–80
Identify and distinguish between common and proper nouns	18–19
Identify pronouns	20
Identify and form singular and plural nouns	21–32
Identify and write plural possessive nouns correctly	33, 35, 39, 41
Identify and write singular possessive nouns correctly	34, 36, 37, 38, 40, 42
Identify and distinguish between subject and object pronouns	43–47
Form different verb tenses	48–62
Choose or write the correct verb tense for the context	48–55
Form verb tenses with irregular verbs	49–53, 56–59, 61–62
Identify and use action verbs	63–66
Identify and use helping verbs	67–70
Recognize that one word can be different parts of speech, depending on its use	78–80

Grammar & Usage Test # 2:

SENTENCES

Test Location: pages 66–67

Skill	Test Items
Identify and distinguish among complete sentences, sentence fragments, and run-on sentences	1–5
Identify and distinguish among simple, compound, and complex sentences	6–10
Identify and distinguish among declarative, imperative, exclamatory, and interrogative sentences	11–14
Identify the simple subject of a sentence	15–17
Identify the simple predicate of a sentence	18–20
Rearrange words within a sentence for clear meaning	21–24
Identify the complete subject of a sentence	25–27
Identify the complete predicate of a sentence	28–30

Grammar & Usage Test # 3:

CAPITALIZATION & PUNCTUATION

Test Location: pages 68–71

Grammar & Usage Test # 4:

LANGUAGE USAGE

Test Location: pages 72–75

Fifth Grade Book of Language Tests

PARTS OF SPEECH

Name _____   Possible Correct Answers: 80

Date _____   Your Correct Answers: _____

Identify the parts of speech in the sentences below by writing . . .

N *for noun*   **V** *for verb*   **AJ** *for adjective*   **AD** *for adverb*

> Three hungry campers gobbled pancakes greedily.

_____ 1. Three   _____ 4. pancakes

_____ 2. gobbled   _____ 5. campers

_____ 3. hungry   _____ 6. greedily

> A wild thunderstorm with spectacular lightning moved rapidly across the lake toward Camp Lookout.

_____ 7. wild   _____ 9. moved   _____ 11. across

_____ 8. thunderstorm   _____ 10. rapidly   _____ 12. lightning

Read this sentence.

> Freddy's ghost story frightened even the oldest campers.

13. Which words are used as nouns? _____

14. Which word is used as a verb? _____

15. Which words are used as adjectives? _____

Read this sentence.

> Didn't the hurried campers notice the fire ants heading for Chucky's sleeping bag?

16. What part of speech is the word *hurried?*

_____

17. What part of speech is the word *Chucky's?*

_____

62

Read the following sentence and look for the nouns. Decide if the nouns are common or proper.

Last Friday, Billy put spiders in our beds, and Spanish moss in the stew.

18. Write the common nouns from the sentence.

_____

19. Write the proper nouns from the sentence.

_____

20. Write the pronouns from the sentence.

_____

Write the plural form of each word below.

_____ 21. compass

_____ 22. knife

_____ 23. tomato

_____ 24. deer

_____ 25. family

_____ 26. bush

Write the singular form of each word below.

_____ 27. mice

_____ 28. children

_____ 29. cities

_____ 30. geese

_____ 31. women

_____ 32. brothers-in-law

Write a possessive noun phrase (2 words) to fit each of Freddy's descriptions.

33. _____

34. _____

35. _____

36. _____

37. _____

38. _____

39. _____

40. _____

41. _____

42. _____

33. teeth belonging to more than one fox
34. chocolate belonging to one mouse
35. shirts belonging to 3 campers
36. teeth belonging to one fox
37. tasty legs of one frog
38. tail of one skunk
39. tent of 2 counselors
40. honk of one goose
41. screams of children
42. roar of a waterfall

Name _____

63

Write the subject pronoun from each sentence.

_____ 43. They couldn't decide where to pitch their tent.

_____ 44. "This is too hard," she said to me.

_____ 45. We agreed that the tent was broken.

Write the object pronoun from each sentence.

_____ 46. You could ask us for help.

_____ 47. We gave them some extra tent poles.

Write the correct form (tense) of the verb needed in each sentence.
(The verb is at the end of each sentence.)

_____ 48. Yesterday, Carl _____ boats for a contest. *(row)*

_____ 49. Today, Lisa _____ away from the sinking boat. *(swim)*

_____ 50. Oh no! Matt _____ off his raft into the river! *(fall)*

_____ 51. Tomorrow our cabin _____ kites. *(fly)*

_____ 52. Who _____ my green pajamas last night? *(wear)*

_____ 53. How many campers _____ to their parents this week? *(write)*

_____ 54. She _____ when she saw the lizard in her shoe. *(faint)*

_____ 55. Last night we _____ to replace the cook. *(vote)*

Find the bold verb in each sentence. Write its present tense.

56. Our counselors **told** us to rest before the climb.

57. Some campers **thought** the hike would be easy.

58. Wow! **Were** they ever wrong about that!

59. All the hikers **found** out they were out of shape.

60. Thankfully, they **stopped** to look for berries.

61. Then they rested and **ate** candy bars.

62. "Wasn't that an amazing bear we **saw**?" they bragged.

56. _____
57. _____
58. _____
59. _____
60. _____
61. _____
62. _____

Name _____

64

Write the action verb from each sentence.

_____ 63. Lisa screamed at the top of her lungs when she saw the face!

_____ 64. She was there when the curtain wiggled.

_____ 65. Lisa crept underneath the covers and stayed there a long time.

_____ 66. Was there a face in the window, or did she imagine it?

Write the helping verb from each sentence.

_____ 67. He is rummaging through the pack, looking for the matches.

_____ 68. Freddy should start getting wood for the campfire before it gets dark.

_____ 69. Shouldn't you be helping Freddy with the firewood?

_____ 70. Is it true that you have seen Bigfoot while you were gathering wood?

Look for the bold word in each sentence. Tell how it is used in the sentence.

Write
**NOUN
VERB
ADJECTIVE**
or
ADVERB
*for each
sentence.*

_____ 71. Eat your grilled **cheese** sandwich.

_____ 72. Watch the song leader **closely**.

_____ 73. Don't you just love the camp **theme** song?

_____ 74. Who won the frog-jumping **contest**?

_____ 75. Counselor Wacky **fell** out of the canoe.

_____ 76. That meat loaf was the most **terrible** food yet!

_____ 77. Back away **slowly** from the rattlesnake.

78. *Sleeping* is used as a verb in sentence _____ and as an adjective in sentence _____ .
   a. We discovered a sleeping bear.
   b. Sleeping under the stars is great fun.

79. *Catch* is used as a verb in sentence _____ and as a noun in sentence _____ .
   a. You made a great catch!
   b. Did you catch any fish?

80. *Stop* is used as an adjective in sentence _____ and as a verb in sentence _____ .
   a. When will you stop putting worms in my bed?
   b. Pay attention to the stop sign.

Name _____

Fifth Grade Book of Language Tests

SENTENCES

Name _____   Possible Correct Answers: 30

Date _____   Your Correct Answers: _____

Decide if each group of words is a complete sentence, fragment, or run-on sentence. Write **C** (for complete), **F** (for fragment), or **R** (for run-on).

_____ 1. Going over the waterfall.

_____ 2. Wear a lifejacket take enough food.

_____ 3. What a cute squirrel in your tent!

_____ 4. Did you step in the poison ivy?

_____ 5. Sneaked into the dining hall at night.

Decide if each sentence is a simple sentence, compound sentence, or complex sentence. Write **S** (for simple), **CD** (for compound), or **CX** (for complex).

_____ 6. Eat your breakfast, and clean your cabins.

_____ 7. After flag raising, we'll play water polo.

_____ 8. Did you try the mystery lunch yet?

_____ 9. Let's swim now because it might rain later.

_____10. Chipmunks are after our food.

Examine each quote from inside the tent. Decide what kind of sentence each is.

_____ 11. Which sentences are declarative?

_____ 12. Which sentences are exclamatory?

_____ 13. Which ones are imperative?

_____ 14. Which ones are interrogative?

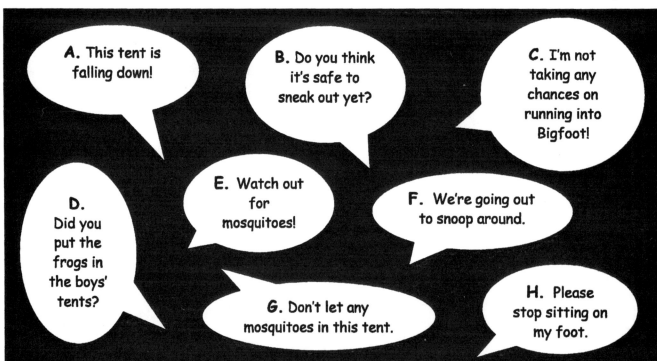

Fifth Grade Book of Language Tests   Copyright ©2000 by Incentive Publications, Inc., Nashville, TN.

Write the simple subject for each sentence on the line beside it.

_____ 15. Sam raced us to the diving board.

_____ 16. Were the bears eating your marshmallows?

_____ 17. The biggest chipmunk took my backpack.

Write the simple predicate for each sentence on the line beside it.

_____ 18. Falling rocks crashed into the campsite.

_____ 19. Could crafty coyotes catch cunning campers?

_____ 20. We watched while the wind blew our tent away.

The meaning of these sentences is confusing because of the order of the words.
Rewrite each sentence so that the meaning is clear.

21. While rowing in a rowboat, a fish jumped up and bit me.

_____

22. I read about a camp counselor who taught scuba diving in a magazine.

_____

23. Hanging from a limb I saw a large snake.

_____

24. While eating the hay, I looked over the horses and decided which one to ride.

_____

Find the complete subject for each sentence. Underline it.

25. After a close race, the tired swimmers headed for the showers.

26. Should the three hungry campers try the chocolate covered ants?

27. Counselors and campers joined together for a tug-of-rope game.

Find the complete predicate for each sentence. Underline it.

28. We have never before seen so many cockroaches in one place!

29. All of us chased them under the bunks and across the floor.

30. Spider webs hang from the corners of our cabin.

Name _____

67

CAPITALIZATION & PUNCTUATION

Name _____

Possible Correct Answers: 50

Date _____

Your Correct Answers: _____

1. Correct the capitalization and punctuation in this letter. Write capital letters over incorrect letters. Add punctuation marks where they are needed. Write other punctuation marks over incorrect ones.
(10 points)

> monday july 14
>
> dear mom and dad
>
> I love being at camp lookout. You wouldn't believe what
> fun I'm having. one of my bunk-mates is from australia,
> and the other one is from the british west indies?
> I ate four hot dogs seven doughboys and six smores on
> our campout do you believe that! Also I have had poison
> ivy all week and I got a snake bite. I love this place
> I have a pet dragonfly could you please send me more
> money for the snack bar.
>   love
>   Maria

2. Circle the words in the sentence below that should have capital letters.

on july fifteenth I traveled to oregon to camp lookout, which is located near the pacific ocean.

2. Circle the words in the sentence below that should have capital letters.

the cook, who was trained in europe, made a delicious french dinner on saturday.

4. Which example has the correct capitalization for this sentence?
   a. The ghost story was so scary that Katya began singing *The Star Spangled Banner.*
   b. The Ghost Story was so scary that katya began singing *the Star Spangled Banner.*
   c. the ghost story was so scary that Katya began singing *the star spangled banner.*

Fifth Grade Book of Language Tests

Copyright ©2000 by Incentive Publications, Inc., Nashville, TN.

Circle the numbers next to titles that are correctly capitalized.
If a title is not correct, make the changes in capitalization that will make it accurate.

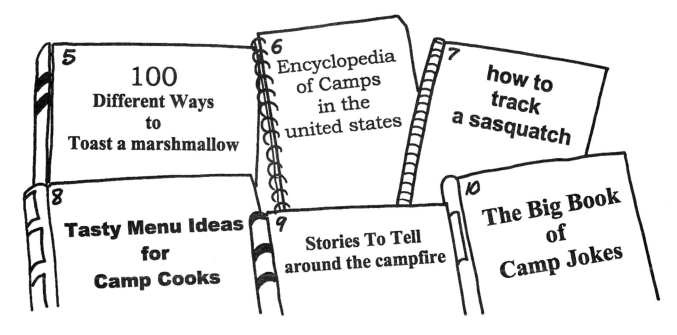

Write the two words that form each contraction.

11. won't _____

12. she'll _____

13. he'd _____

14. weren't _____

15. I've _____

Form a contraction from the two words given.

16. could not _____

17. we have _____

18. they are _____

19. we would _____

20. are not _____

21. Which example shows correct use of commas?

    a. After we ate lunch, on Sunday July 22, we swam went canoeing and raced turtles.

    b. After we ate lunch on Sunday, July 22, we swam, went canoeing, and raced turtles.

    c. After, we ate lunch on Sunday July 22, we swam, went canoeing and raced turtles.

    d. After we ate lunch on Sunday July 22, we swam, went canoeing and raced turtles.

22. Which example shows correct use of commas?

    a. Henri the camp cook, has a lot of trouble controlling Oscar the camp's pet alligator.

    b. Henri, the camp cook, has a lot of trouble, controlling Oscar, the camp's pet alligator.

    c. Henri the camp cook has a lot of trouble controlling Oscar, the camp's pet alligator.

    d. Henri, the camp cook, has a lot of trouble controlling Oscar, the camp's pet alligator.

Name _____

Fifth Grade Book of Language Tests

23. Which sentences in Counselor Jake's Activity Log have correct punctuation?
    Circle the letter of any sentences that are correctly punctuated.

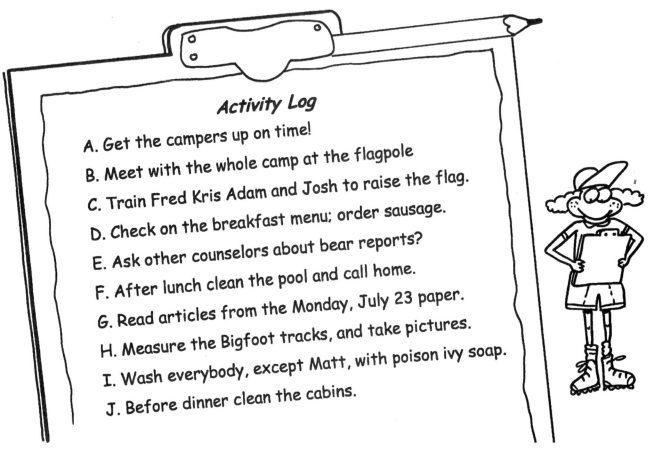

Activity Log

A. Get the campers up on time!

B. Meet with the whole camp at the flagpole

C. Train Fred Kris Adam and Josh to raise the flag.

D. Check on the breakfast menu; order sausage.

E. Ask other counselors about bear reports?

F. After lunch clean the pool and call home.

G. Read articles from the Monday, July 23 paper.

H. Measure the Bigfoot tracks, and take pictures.

I. Wash everybody, except Matt, with poison ivy soap.

J. Before dinner clean the cabins.

Add punctuation to the following sentences.

24. Is it true asked Flo that you ran into a bear on your hike this morning

25. Janice wondered Jim, how many marshmallows did you really eat last night

26. I never should have packed this many clothes Tara complained as she did her laundry

27. At the campfire, Counselor Carla said I notice that Frankie is not here tonight

28. You're not the only camper who's dreading survival training said Michael

29. The food at Camp Lookout bragged the cook is the best in the whole country

30. But I've never sailed a boat before wailed Todd as the wind pushed the boat around

31. We don't really believe your story about the fish Jessica's friends told her

32. The camp director announced There is a big storm coming and we must get ready

Name _____

Fifth Grade Book of Language Tests

The signs on this trail need some fixing. They have many errors in capitalization and punctuation. Write the sign information correctly on each sign. Fix all the errors.

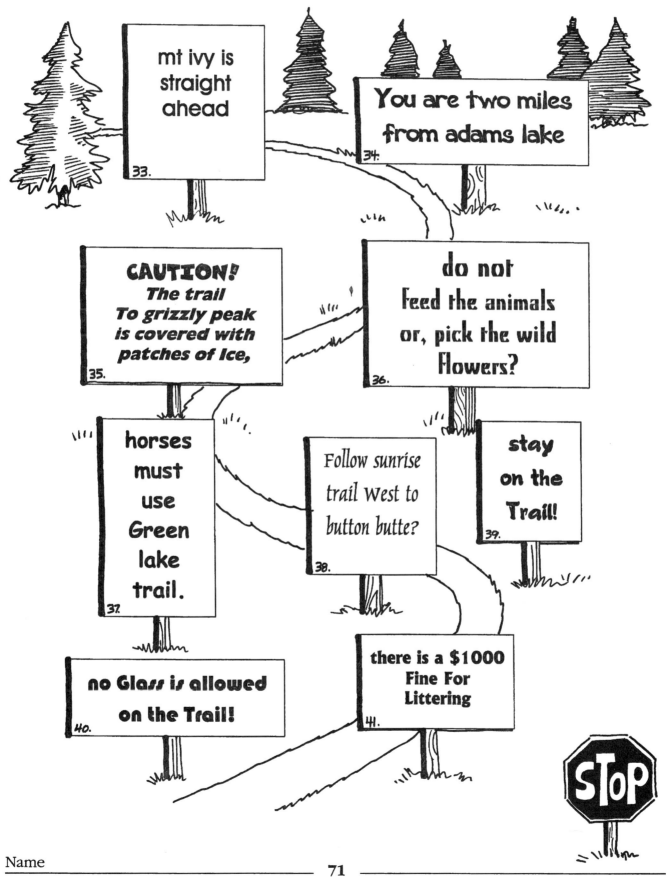

33. mt ivy is straight ahead

34. You are two miles from adams lake

35. CAUTION! The trail To grizzly peak is covered with patches of Ice,

36. do not feed the animals or, pick the wild flowers?

37. horses must use Green lake trail.

38. Follow sunrise trail West to button butte?

39. stay on the Trail!

40. no Glass is allowed on the Trail!

41. there is a $1000 Fine For Littering

STOP

Name

Fifth Grade Book of Language Tests

LANGUAGE USAGE

Name _____　　Possible Correct Answers: 70

Date _____　　Your Correct Answers: _____

Circle the correct form of the verb to agree with the subject of each sentence below.

1. Polly and Penny (has, have) stayed in the same cabin every year.
2. The other campers and I (am, are) supposed to be asleep by ten o'clock.
3. The campers in the end bunk (has, have) been snoring for an hour.
4. Penny (has, have) often fallen out of her bunk.
5. Our counselors (was, were) once campers in this cabin.
6. Both counselors (spend, spends) every summer at Camp Lookout.
7. Every morning, Josh and Jake (raise, raises) the flag before breakfast.
8. Counselor Leo and Counselor Cleo (teach, teaches) us how to swim.
9. The Camp Director (guide, guides) us on the greatest nature hikes.
10. The camp cooks, Henri and Sheri (make, makes) the best waffles.

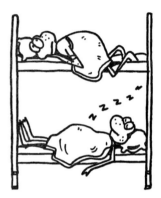

Choose the correct pronoun to agree with the noun in each sentence below.

11. The cooks wanted us to enjoy (their, her) pancakes.
12. After we ate the roast pig, Henri asked how we liked (it, them).
13. Todd and Al invited us to join (him, them) on an after-dinner hike.

14. Which is the correct use of the possessive?
   a. The two counselors ghost story's scared us.
   b. The two counselor's ghost stories scared us.
   c. The two counselors' ghost stories scared us.

15. Which is the correct use of the possessive?
   a. I was terrified by last night's noises.
   b. I was terrified by last night's noise's.
   c. I was terrified by last nights' noises.

16. Which is the correct use of the possessive?
   a. The three girls' flashlight's had burned out.
   b. The three girls' flashlights had burned out.
   c. The three girl's flashlights had burned out.

17. Which is the correct use of the possessive?
   a. Even the wind's whistling was frightening.
   b. Even the winds' whistling was frightening.
   c. Even the winds's whistling was frightening.

72

Choose the correct pronoun for each blank. Write the pronoun.

18. Let's go with _____ to the snack shop. (them, they)

19. Abby says she'll buy Penny and _____ some licorice ropes. (I, me)

20. _____ girls have spent all our snack money already. (Us, We)

21. Counselor Cleo shared his potato chips with _____ and me. (she, her)

22. Sandy and _____ wish we had not used up all our money so soon. (I, me)

23. Which is correct?
   a. Could you learn karate from he and she?
   b. Could you learn karate from him and her?
   c. Could you learn karate from he and her?
   d. Could you learn karate from him and she?

24. Which is correct?
   a. Me and him already took karate lessons.
   b. Him and I already took karate lessons.
   c. I and he already took karate lessons.
   d. He and I already took karate lessons.

25. Circle the letters of the sentences that use negatives correctly.

A. Aren't you never coming along to search for Bigfoot?
B. Couldn't you never believe in Bigfoot?
C. Haven't you taken any pictures yet?
D. No, we tried, but couldn't get no pictures.
E. We have got nothing to do but search.
F. No one wouldn't want to miss a chance to see Bigfoot.
G. Dan, don't you and Al never want to come with us?
H. We don't ever want to go into that forest again.

Circle the word that correctly completes each sentence below.

26. I've gotten a little (horse, hoarse) from yelling at you across the field.

27. Is (there, their, they're) any way you can join me to ride horses tonight?

28. Let's (meet, meat) at the horse stables at exactly midnight.

29. The twins said we could ride (there, they're, their) horses tonight.

30. Watch out! (Your, You're) horse is about to step in a huge (hole, whole)!

31. We're lost, we've (been, bin) riding in circles and I can't (see, sea) the stables.

Name _____

73

Fifth Grade Book of Language Tests

Every notice on the camp bulletin board has an error in language usage.
Find each error, cross it out, and fix the sentence!

32. The weather looks well today.

33. Congratulations! You all did good on the midnight hike.

34. Today our campers showed that they may all swim well!

35. Who missed J.J.'s scary stories? You would of loved them!

36. Don't let your sleeping bags out in the rain.

37. Everyone should of come with us to the tar pits!

38. We'll leave everyone sleep in on Saturday morning.

39. I can learn anyone how to yodel. Contact me for lessons. Patsy

40. Don't set too close to the edge of the bluff.

41. Can I borrow someone's compass? See me at Cabin 10. Jamie

42. Don't sit your sleeping bag too close to the fire.

43. I'm looking for someone to set with me at the rodeo. Pete

44. It's well that you're all here at Camp Lookout!

45. Isn't it amazing how Jamie he got away from that bear?

46. Doesn't everyone feel well about the talent show?

47. The comet it will appear about midnight.

Write the correct form of the adjective that should be placed in each blank.
The adjectives are shown at the end of each sentence.

48. Karl's frog raced _____ than Isaac's. (fast)

49. Whose frog jumped the _____ ? (farther)

50. This is the _____ frog I've ever seen! (slimy)

Write the adverb form that will correctly fill the blank.

51. Billy gets up _____ than the other campers. (early)

52. He plays pranks the _____ of all the campers. (often)

53. The raccoons behaved _____ tonight than any other night. (strange)

Choose the adjective that correctly fills the blank. Circle it.

54. This is _____ pizza than what we had last night. (better, best)

55. I've eaten a lot, but it's still _____ than you've eaten. (less, least)

56. My score was the _____ of all the runners. (worse, worst)

Write the preposition from each sentence.

57. What is hidden under your bed? _____

58. Stay away from the skunks. _____

59. Let's push the counselors into the pool. _____

60. I'll race you across the campground. _____

Write the prepositional phrase from each sentence.

_____ 61. Don't go sailing without a life jacket!

_____ 62. During the night, a coon ate your toothpaste.

_____ 63. There's some rotten food beneath your bed.

_____ 64. Also, there are spiders hanging above your head.

_____ 65. Leave your wet clothes outside the door.

Circle the direct object in each sentence.

66. Let's go down to the river and dig some worms.

67. Grab your towels and run!

68. After dinner, we'll play some good pranks on the boys.

69. The worms might cause some commotion.

70. What a great way to enjoy our last night!

Name _____

75

Fifth Grade Book of Language Tests

Words & Vocabulary Skills Checklists

Words & Vocabulary Test # 1:

WORD PARTS

Test Location: pages 78–79

Skill	*Test Items*
Identify the meanings of common prefixes	1–15
Recognize and use prefixes to determine word meaning	16–34
Identify the meanings of common suffixes	35–42
Recognize and use suffixes to determine word meaning	43–52
Identify the meanings of common roots	53–63
Recognize and use roots to determine meanings of words	64–67
Recognize compound words	68–70

Words & Vocabulary Test # 2:

VOCABULARY WORD MEANINGS

Test Location: pages 80–83

Skill	*Test Items*
Show understanding of word meaning by answering questions about word use	1–5
Recognize meanings and definitions of words	6–15
Recognize and use synonyms	16–20
Recognize and use antonyms	21–25
Use context clues to determine a word's meaning	26–29
Choose the correct word for a particular context	30–33
Identify words with similar meanings	34–37
Distinguish between the denotation and connotation of a word	38–39
Identify a word from its denotation and connotation	40–41
Identify and define words with multiple meanings	42–45

Words & Vocabulary Test # 3:

CONFUSING WORDS

Test Location: pages 84–87

Fifth Grade Book of Language Tests

WORD PARTS

Name _____

Possible Correct Answers: 70

Date _____

Your Correct Answers: _____

supervisor	preview
ashore	improper
octagon	antibiotic
mistake	regain
expel	miniature
uniform	maximum
centipede	semicircle
transport	submerge

Beside each numbered word below, write a word from the poster above that has a prefix meaning the same as the numbered word.

1. before _____
2. small _____
3. against _____
4. hundred _____
5. wrong _____
6. across _____
7. one _____
8. not _____
9. under _____
10. on _____
11. again _____
12. half _____
13. out _____
14. eight _____
15. above _____

Add a prefix to each word below to form a word that fits the meaning in parentheses.

16. _____ cycle   (two wheels)
17. _____ operate   (operate together)
18. _____ war   (after the war)
19. _____ read   (read wrong)
20. _____ approve   (not approve)
21. _____ hale   (breathe out)
22. _____ consistent (not consistent)
23. _____ chip   (tiny chip)
24. _____ field   (middle of the field)
25. _____ stop   (without a stop)
26. _____ human   (above human)
27. _____ cycle   (one circle or wheel)
28. _____ agon   (five-sided figure)
29. _____ function   (function wrong)
30. _____ atlantic   (across the Atlantic)
31. _____ write   (write again)
32. _____ write   (write together)
33. _____ complete   (half complete)
34. _____ freeze   (against freezing)

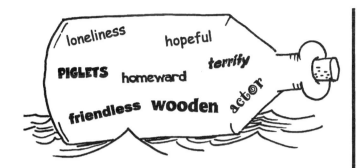

Write the word found on the bottle that has a *suffix* which means:

35. one who _____

36. to cause to be _____

37. full of _____

38. without _____

39. small _____

40. made of _____

41. toward _____

42. a condition of _____

Add a *suffix* to form a word that fits each meaning in parentheses.

43. peril _____ (full of peril)

44. storm _____ (like a storm)

45. hope _____ (without hope)

46. trouble _____ (full of trouble)

47. back _____ (towards the back)

48. sail _____ (one who sails)

49. silk _____ (made of silk)

50. drop _____ (little drops)

51. coward _____ (like a coward)

52. friend _____ (state of being friends)

Find a word from the list having a root to match each meaning. Write the letter of the word.

53. _____earth

54. _____high

55. _____water

56. _____self

57. _____power

58. _____break

59. _____year

60. _____moon

61. _____move

62. _____fear

63. _____time

A. aqueduct
B. fracture
C. arachnaphobia
D. fugitive
E. temporary
F. annual
G. flammable
H. descend
I. geology
J. lunar
K. solar
L. acrobat
M. dynamite
N. transfer
O. autograph

Find a word from the list to match each meaning. Write the letter of the word.

64. ___ related to the sun

65. ___ climb down

66. ___ can be burned

67. ___ one who flees

Circle the compound words in each group.

68. tricycle
waterfall
transcript
submarine
seaside

69. candlestick
transport
seasick
shipwreck
sunstroke

70. automatic
acrobat
fireside
swimsuit
surfboard

Name

79

Fifth Grade Book of Language Tests

VOCABULARY WORD MEANINGS

Name _____

Date _____

Possible Correct Answers: 45

Your Correct Answers: _____

1. Which would you find in the ocean?

   a sequoia   flotsam   an eclipse   a bungalow

2. Which would you choose to help you sail a ship?

   a mariner   a novice   a manatee   a euphonium

3. Which of these would you eat?

   a vessel   a grotto   a foible   a borscht

4. Which would you be likely to find in a church?

   a vicar   a quadruped   a subpoena   a barracuda

5. Would you probably find words in a lexicon?

   yes   no

Write the word from the picture below that matches each definition.

_____ 6. foe

_____ 7. friendly

_____ 8. scold

_____ 9. gloomy

_____ 10. scoundrel

_____ 11. lie

_____ 12. very hungry

_____ 13. whirlpool

_____ 14. odor

_____ 15. on time

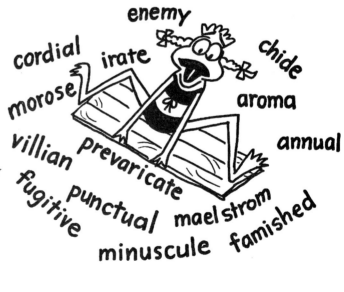

enemy
cordial   irate   chide
morose   aroma
villian   prevaricate   annual
fugitive   punctual   maelstrom
minuscule   famished

80

16. Which word is a synonym for **novice**?
    a. veteran   c. beginner
    b. professional   d. noticeable

17. Which word is a synonym for **valiant**?
    a. wise   c. scary
    b. valuable   d. brave

18. Which word is a synonym for **obstinate**?
    a. stubborn   c. fearful
    b. old-fashioned   d. youthful

19. Which word is a synonym for **concealed**?
    a. water-tight   c. confused
    b. hidden   d. spoiled

20. Which word is a synonym for **foible**?
    a. flaw   c. accident
    b. unstable   d. blemish

Search this book to find an antonym for each word below.
Write each word on the proper line.

_____ 21. cordial

_____ 22. sturdy

_____ 23. careless

_____ 24. accelerated

_____ 25. temporary

permanent
flimsy
rude
speedy

friendly
heavy
cautious
agony
slowed

Use the *context* of each bold word in questions 26 and 27 to decide what the word means.

26. I had never seen a bathing suit quite like the **peculiar** one she wore yesterday.

    I think this word means: _____

27. The **ambidextrous** girl wrote one letter with her left hand and one with her right hand.

    I think this word means: _____

Name _____

28. Warm sunshine, a soft ocean breeze, and a cushioned beach chair
produce a setting conducive to relaxation.

   In the sentence above, *conducive* means
   a. opposite from b. harmful c. promoting d. prohibiting

29. The tortuous road to the beach caused Mario
to have a very queasy stomach.

   In the sentence above, *tortuous* means
   a. dangerous b. winding c. washed-out d. frightening

Use context clues to choose the word that best fits in each sentence below.
Write each word in the proper blank.

30. We laughed when the crab _____ Brad's goggles.
   disappeared   snatched   returned   crawled

31. I was surprised by the _____ of a lifeguard on this
   crowded beach.
   presence   hairdo   tan   absence

32. Jamie was hurt by Amy's _____ remarks about her
   new swimsuit.
   courteous   crude   careful   creative

33. Jake was _____ when he saw how close the shark was
   to his surfboard.
   horrific   satisfied   terrified   horrible

34. Circle the word that does NOT have a meaning similar to the others.
   anxious   disturbed
   nervous   calm

35. Circle the word that does NOT have a meaning similar to the others.
   proceed   halt
   stop   cease

36. Circle the word that does NOT have a meaning similar to the others.
   tense   taught
   tender   tight

Name _____

Fifth Grade Book of Language Tests

37. Circle the word that does NOT have a meaning similar to the others.

    abrupt   sudden   hasty   tranquil

38. Circle the connotation of the word *pirate*.
    a. one who robs ships at sea
    b. a mean, ruthless man with a patched eye and a wooden leg who makes people walk the plank off a ship into the ocean

39. Circle the denotation of the word *surf*.
    a. the foamy, breaking waves that are such fun for swimming and jumping
    b. the swelling of the sea that breaks on the shore

40. Read the denotation and connotation. Tell what the word is. _____
    Denotation: .... the breaking up of a sea-going vessel
    Connotation: .... the crashing and splitting apart of a boat into rocks on a wild sea

41. Read the denotation and connotation. Tell what the word is. _____
    Denotation: .... irritation or blistering caused by exposure to the sun
    Connotation: .... miserable, painful, red skin that you can't stand to touch

42. Read these two meanings of a word. What is the word? _____
    a. to remove from a job
    b. something that burns

43. Read these two meanings of a word. What is the word? _____
    a. a place to run a race
    b. animal footprint

44. Read these two meanings of a word. What is the word? _____
    a. to see something
    b. a dot on a ladybug

45. Read these two meanings of a word.
    What is the word? _____
    a. to ride a bike without pedaling
    b. the edge of a continent

Name _____

83

Fifth Grade Book of Language Tests

CONFUSING WORDS

Name _____   Possible Correct Answers: 75

Date _____   Your Correct Answers: _____

Choose the correct homonym to complete each sentence.

1. Who would like to be _____ (buried, berried) in the sand?

2. I _____ (heard, herd) about your surfing accident.

3. Let's clean up the junk people _____ (through, threw) on the beach today.

4. My boat's motor died, so my friends _____ (toad, towed) it back to shore.

5. Oh, no! She's headed _____ (strait, straight) for the shark!

6. Is it true that you've _____ (cot, caught) twenty crabs today?

7. The tide is rising and your _____ (close, clothes) will get wet if you
   don't move them!

8. Amanda let out a _____ (groan, grown) when she started feeling her sunburn.

9. Who _____ (taut, taught) you how to handle that sailboat so skillfully?

10. You really do _____ (need, knead) to get some sunscreen on your body!

In each of the nine signs above, there is at least one word that is a homonym. Write another
homonym (a different spelling) for one of the homonyms on each sign.

11. _____   14. _____   17. _____

12. _____   15. _____   18. _____

13. _____   16. _____   19. _____

Fifth Grade Book of Language Tests

Circle the word that is the correct one for each sentence.

20. Hurry! Run! A (meteor, meteorite) has just hit the beach!

21. Did that lotion have any (effect, affect) on the pain of your sunburn?

22. Juna was offered a lifeguard job, but decided not to (accept, except) it.

23. Roberto never (attended, intended) to be snorkeling in shark-infested waters.

24. Was Landra flattered by the (complaint, compliment) about her surfing skills?

25. The kids did a very (thorough, through) job of cleaning the trash off the beach.

26. The lifeguard told Sam, "I'd (advice, advise) you to get out of the sun right away."

27. After last year's hurricane, Jerod's family decided to buy flood (insurance, assurance).

28. The sea glass was so clear and (translucent, transparent) that we could see through it easily.

29. The volleyball players were (altogether, all together) satisfied with the new volleyball nets.

Choose the correct word from the sign to complete each sentence. Write the word.

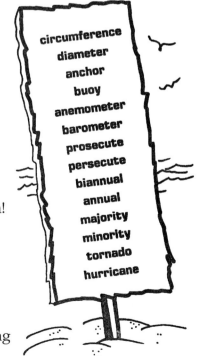

circumference
diameter
anchor
buoy
anemometer
barometer
prosecute
persecute
biannual
annual
majority
minority
tornado
hurricane

30. Jane painted a stripe around the _____ of her beach ball.

31. When the ship reached port, the captain dropped the _____ .

32. The lifeguard used a _____ to measure the speed of the wind at the beach.

33. Don't _____ those poor little sand crabs on the beach!

34. I've played in the _____ beach volleyball tournament every year for the past ten years.

35. Since the _____ of the players want to start in the morning, the game will begin at 9:00 A.M.

36. It's time to leave the beach. A violent _____ is heading across the water and is supposed to hit the coast tomorrow.

Name _____

85

Four of the five words in each group below are related in some way.
Cross out the unrelated word in each group.

37.	anemone	barracuda	lobster	crocodile	squid
38.	sunshine	flashlight	boardwalk	butterfly	camera
39.	mice	artichoke	rainbows	keys	babies
40.	clavicle	femur	kneecap	liver	spine
41.	blizzard	hurricane	tornado	tomato	cyclone
42.	blizzard	fizzy	zipper	buzzard	fuzzy

Below is a description of the history and origin of seven words.
Write the word that matches each one.
Choose from the words on the boat's sail.

_____ 43. from a Greek word meaning **long-tailed star**

_____ 44. a Latin word meaning **head**

_____ 45. a word meaning **day of the moon**

_____ 46. a dog named after a state in Mexico

_____ 47. from New Latin, meaning **eight-footed**

_____ 48. a Persian garment with legs and feet

_____ 49. from a Greek word
meaning **messenger**

words on sail: angel, octopus, comet, pajama, Monday, sardine, lasagna, march, Chihuahua, cabbage, cologne

Match these food words of foreign origin with their meanings.
Write each word on the lines below.

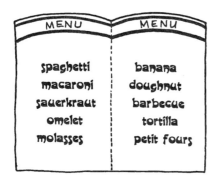

MENU: spaghetti, macaroni, sauerkraut, omelet, molasses, banana, doughnut, barbecue, tortilla, petit fours

51. from French —
meaning **thin plate**

_____

52. from Spanish —
meaning a **round cake**

_____

53. from Portuguese —
meaning **honey**

_____

54. from French — meaning
little cakes

_____

55. from Italian — meaning
a **round swelling**

_____

56. from Italian —
meaning **string**

_____

50. from German —
meaning **sour cabbage**

_____

Name _____

Write the letter of the figure of speech that matches each meaning below.

_____ 57. calm down

_____ 58. show your feelings easily

_____ 59. say something embarrassing

_____ 60. an argument to have

_____ 61. makes you mad

_____ 62. give away a secret

_____ 63. take a chance

_____ 64. a bad deal, full of problems

_____ 65. is very expensive

_____ 66. start too soon

_____ 67. fool around

_____ 68. want to back out

a. spill the beans
b. get cold feet
c. jump the gun
d. cost an arm and a leg
e. red letter day
f. a real lemon
g. in mint condition
h. a bone to pick
i . cooks your goose
j. knock it off
k. go out on a limb
l. scream bloody murder
m. keep a lid on it
n. wear your heart on your sleeve
o. put your foot in your mouth
p. ham it up

Finish these analogies.

69. legs : crab   **as**   _____ : octopus

70. motorcycle : motorcycles   **as**   _____ : geese

71. _____ : mice   **as**   child : children

72. melt : _____   **as**   compliment : complaint

73. _____ : blizzard   **as**   rain : monsoon

74. argue : _____   **as**   excite : excitement

75. calculator : mathematician

        as surfboard : _____

Name _____

87

Study & Research Skills Checklists

Study & Research Test # 1:

DICTIONARY & ENCYCLOPEDIA SKILLS

Test Location: pages 90–93

Skill	*Test Items*
Recognize and put names in alphabetical order	1, 4, 7
Recognize and put words in alphabetical order	2–3
Recognize and put phrases in alphabetical order	5
Recognize and put titles in alphabetical order	6–8
Use guide words to locate items in a dictionary	9–25
Use guide words to locate items in an encyclopedia	26–33
Identify key words for finding information in an encyclopedia	34–37
Use a dictionary to find information about words other than meanings	38, 39, 41, 43, 44
Use a dictionary to find word meanings	40, 42
Find information in an encyclopedia entry	45–50

Study & Research Test # 2:

REFERENCE & INFORMATION SKILLS

Test Location: pages 94–99

Skill	*Test Items*
Identify the uses of a variety of reference materials	1–11
Select the best reference material for an information-gathering task	12–32
Identify the purposes of various parts of a book	33–38
Find and interpret information in a Table of Contents	39–46
Find and interpret information in an index	47–53
Find and interpret information in an illustration	54–55
Find and interpret information on a map	56–60
Find and interpret information on a timeline	61–66
Find and interpret information on charts, tables, and graphs	67–75

Fifth Grade Book of Language Tests

Study & Research Test # 3:

LIBRARY SKILLS

Test Location: pages 100–101

Skill	*Test Items*
Distinguish between fiction, nonfiction, and biography	1–2
Show understanding of the library system for classifying nonfiction	3
Show understanding of the library system for classifying fiction	4
Understand use of author, title, and subject cards or screen in a library catalog	5
Understand how to use a library catalog to locate books	6
Find information on library cards	7–15
Show familiarity with the Dewey Decimal System	16–25
Use the Dewey Decimal System to locate books	16–25

Study & Research Test # 4:

STUDY SKILLS

Test Location: pages 102–103

Skill	*Test Items*
Form good questions to gain information	1
Gain information quickly by skimming a passage	2–4
Identify the main idea in a passage	5
Identify ideas in a passage that support the main point	6
Summarize a passage	7
Use an outline to organize information	8–10

Fifth Grade Book of Language Tests

DICTIONARY & ENCYCLOPEDIA SKILLS

Name _____

Possible Correct Answers: 50

Date _____

Your Correct Answers: _____

1. Help Detective Bea Sharp with her search for a cleaning service. Number these business names 1 to 5 in the correct alphabetical order.

   ____ Myster's Maids

   ____ Monster Cleaning, Inc.

   ____ Missy's Mop Service

   ____ Myers' Messy Clean-Up

   ____ Moe's Clean-as-a-Whistle, Inc.

2. Which of the following groups is in alphabetical order?
   a. detective, daily, decide, detect, double
   b. daily, decide, detect, detective, double
   c. daily, double, decide, detective, detect

3. Which of the following groups is in alphabetical order?
   a. ghost, gaggle, ghastly, grouchy, gag
   b. gag, gaggle, ghastly, grouchy, ghost
   c. gag, gaggle, ghastly, ghost, grouchy

4. Which of the following groups is in alphabetical order?
   a. Cincinnati, Columbus, Columbia, Chicago
   b. Chicago, Cincinnati, Columbia, Columbus
   c. Chicago, Cincinnati, Columbus, Columbia

5. Number these phrases 1–5 in alphabetical order.

   ____ out of order

   ____ out in left field

   ____ out of this world

   ____ out to lunch

   ____ outside the beltway

6. Number these titles 1–5 in alphabetical order.

   ____ *The Case of the Missing Doughnuts*

   ____ *The Case of the Missing Microchip*

   ____ *The Curious Case of the Internet Spies*

   ____ *The Case of the Disappearing Chefs*

   ____ *The Challenging Case of the Lost Teeth*

7. Number these names 1–5 in alphabetical order.

   ____ Sahara Desert

   ____ Saint Helen's Mountain

   ____ Saint Lawrence River

   ____ San Francisco Bay

   ____ Salt Lake City

8. Number these titles 1–5 in alphabetical order.

   ____ *Where in the World is Sri Lanka?*

   ____ *Where in the World is Oliver Ornsby?*

   ____ *Whatever Happened to Henry?*

   ____ *Which Way to Bora Bora?*

   ____ *Where in the World is My Dinner?*

Use these dictionary guide words to answer questions 9–25.

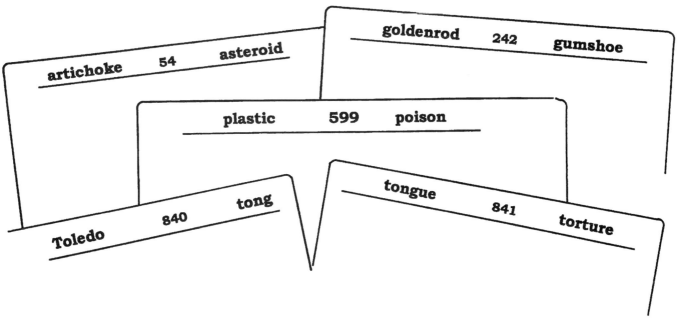

artichoke   54   asteroid

goldenrod   242   gumshoe

plastic   599   poison

Toledo   840   tong

tongue   841   torture

9. Could **tangerine** be found on one of these pages?_____

10. Would **grunion** be found on page 242? _____

11. On what page would you find **torque?** _____

12. Would **pogo stick** be found on page 599?_____

13. On what page would you find **tomato**? _____

14. Would **pneumonia** be found on page 599?_____

15. On what page would you find **torment**? _____

16. Would **pianist** be found on page 599? _____

17. Would **golfer** be found on page 242? _____

18. Would **aardvark** be found on one of these pages?_____

19. Would **artificial** be found on page 54?_____

20. Would **astronaut** be found on page 54?_____

21. Would **asparagus** be found on one of these pages?_____

22. On what page would you find **guffaw**? _____

23. On what page would you find **tornado**? _____

24. Would **goggles** be found on one of these pages? _____

25. On what page would you find **tonsils**? _____

Name _____

91

Fifth Grade Book of Language Tests

Use these encyclopedia guide words to answer questions 26–33.

| Egypt | 290 | electrode |

| Internal Revenue Service | 1490 | Irish Language |

| Lilly, John | 2001 | luminosity |

| macadamia nut | 2270 | machine tool |

_____ 26. Would *electron microscope* be found on page 290?

_____ 27. Would *internal combustion engine* be found on page 1490?

_____ 28. Would the *lymph system* be found on page 2001?

_____ 29. Would *macaroni* be found on page 2270?

_____ 30. Would *irrigation* be found on page 1490?

_____ 31. Would *Macbeth* be found on page 2270?

_____ 32. Would *electoral college* be found on page 290?

_____ 33. Would *Lunar Rover* be found on page 2001?

Which is the best key word or phrase to use when searching in the encyclopedia for each of these topics?

34. Name of the capital of Belgium

    Europe   Belgium   capitals   cities   countries

35. How a telescope works

    telescope   astronomy   science   space

36. Names of characters in William Shakespeare's play, Hamlet

    William   theater   English   Hamlet   plays

37. The size of the Everglades Swamp in southern Florida

    Everglades   swamps   Florida   United States   alligators

Name _____

Use this dictionary entry to answer questions 38–44.

DICTIONARY

de-tect (dǐ-těkt') *v.* –tected, -tecting, -tects. 1. To discover or find the existence of something or fact of something. 2. To find out the truth about something. 3. *Electronics.* To demodulate or extract information from a modulated carrier wave. [Middle English *detecten* from Latin *detegere*, to uncover.] –de-tect-a-ble, de-tect-ible *adj.* –de-tect-er *n.*

38. What part of speech is this word?

_____

39. From what language does this word come?

_____

40. How many meanings are shown in this entry?

_____

41. Write the past tense of this word.

_____

42. Which of the three meanings is used in the following sentence? *(Circle 1, 2, or 3.)*

Do I detect a bit of grumpiness in you today?

   1   **2**   **3**

43. Write the adjective form of this word.

_____

44. What is the meaning of the Latin relative of this word?

_____

Use this encyclopedia entry to finish sentences 45–50.

ENCYCLOPEDIA

comet—A comet looks like a giant beam or ball of light with a long tail, speeding through the night sky. Comets contain a solid nucleus made of ice. The nucleus is surrounded by a bluish cloud layer, or coma, made of gases including carbon monoxide, water vapor, and nitrogen. The long tail contains dust grains and ions of carbon monoxide. The tail glows because sunlight reflects off the grains. The tail of a comet always points away from the sun.

    Comets orbit the sun. A comet can be seen from Earth when its orbit crosses Earth's orbit. Comets are named after their discoverers.

45. A comet's nucleus is made of

_____ .

46. The tail of a comet points

_____ .

47. The cloud around the nucleus is the

_____ .

48. A comet is named after

_____ .

49. The tail glows because

_____ .

50. The comet's tail is made of

_____ .

Name _____

93

REFERENCE & INFORMATION SKILLS

Name _____

Possible Correct Answers: 75

Date _____

Your Correct Answers: _____

Below are descriptions of different reference books.
Match them with the names of the reference books on the detective's notepad.

Write the number of the description on the line before the correct book name.
(One book name is not described below.)

REFERENCE BOOKS to REMEMBER

_____ *almanac*   _____ *book of quotations*

_____ *dictionary*   _____ *biographical dictionary*

_____ *atlas*   _____ *newspaper*

_____ *encyclopedia*   _____ *geographical dictionary*

_____ *thesaurus*   _____ *telephone directory*

_____ *timeline*   _____ *book of records*

1. a collection of words and their synonyms

2. a book that is published yearly, containing a variety of general and numerical information

3. a collection of news, articles, opinions, features, and advertising published daily or weekly

4. a collection of words arranged alphabetically, and information about the words' meanings, uses, forms, pronunciations, and histories

5. a collection of information in one or more volumes on many subjects, gathered together in articles that are alphabetically arranged

6. a book of current records of sporting events and various other events and accomplishments

7. a book of interesting or important statements that have been made

8. an alphabetical listing of the names of places in the world and their descriptions and locations

9. a collection of maps bound into a book

10. a sequential list of events represented by a diagram arranged by dates

11. a collection of articles telling about the lives of people and their accomplishments, arranged alphabetically

Which reference should you use to find each of the following kinds of information?

Choose the best reference for each task from Gary Gumshoe's list.
Write the letter of the reference on the line beside the task.

_____ 12. a history of the word **pirate**

_____ 13. the titles of some books by the author, Mark Twain

_____ 14. five words that mean the same as **terrified**

_____ 15. the location of Istanbul

_____ 16. the title of a book of poetry by Maya Angelou

_____ 17. the history of the Loch Ness Monster

_____ 18. a synonym for the word **obstreperous**

_____ 19. a list of private detectives in your area

_____ 20. the correct pronunciation of the word **hors d'oeurves**

_____ 21. the author of the book, <u>James and the Giant Peach</u>

_____ 22. the present population of Texas

_____ 23. the climate of New Zealand

_____ 24. products produced in Liberia

_____ 25. a weather forecast for tomorrow in your city

_____ 26. a weather forecast for tomorrow in Paris, France

_____ 27. the cost of a book about Harry Potter

_____ 28. which volume of an encyclopedia
has information about black holes

_____ 29. a good hotel in Sydney, Australia

_____ 30. the latest Olympic Gold medalist in men's figure skating

_____ 31. a short biography of Elizabeth Dole

_____ 32. the name of the current record holder for cricket-spitting

A. atlas

B. almanac

C. biographical dictionary

D. dictionary

E. encyclopedia

F. encyclopedia index

G. geographical dictionary

H. <u>Guinness Book of Records</u>

I. Internet

J. library catalog

K. newspaper

L. recipe book

M. telephone directory

N. thesaurus

Name _____

95

Fifth Grade Book of Language Tests

Write the book part that matches each of the definitions in questions 33–38.

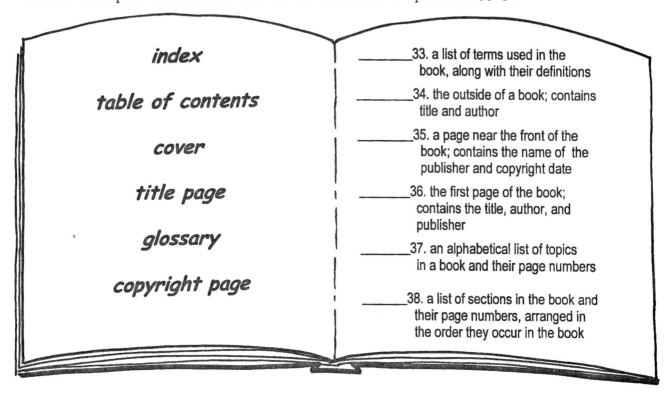

index

table of contents

cover

title page

glossary

copyright page

_____33. a list of terms used in the book, along with their definitions

_____34. the outside of a book; contains title and author

_____35. a page near the front of the book; contains the name of the publisher and copyright date

_____36. the first page of the book; contains the title, author, and publisher

_____37. an alphabetical list of topics in a book and their page numbers

_____38. a list of sections in the book and their page numbers, arranged in the order they occur in the book

Use this Table of Contents to answer questions 39–46.

Table of Contents

39. On which pages would you find cases involving animals? _____

40. What pages cover break-ins and burglaries? _____

41. Which chapter is the longest? _____

42. Which pages cover a graduation ceremony? _____

43. On what page can you begin reading about a case that took place in a deserted house? _____

44. Where can you read about a case involving food? _____

45. How many pages cover the fingerprint case? _____

46. How many pages cover the Recycling Center Robbery? _____

Name _____

Fifth Grade Book of Language Tests

Copyright ©2000 by Incentive Publications, Inc., Nashville, TN.

Use this Index for questions 47–53.

INDEX

Animal Hospital, 57-61
Anonymous Bank Deposit, 84-92
Backwards Graduation
    Ceremony, 70-77
Bank Deposit, 84-93
Bathtub Ring, 93-99
Break-Ins
    Shoelace Factory, 54-56
    Animal Hospital, 57-61
Burglaries
    Fingerprints, 48-53
    Recycling Center, 62-67

Chocolate Eclairs, 40-45
Choosing Cases, 6-11
Circus Train, 26-31
Deserted House, 93-99
Disappearances
    Circus Train, 26-31
    Chocolate Eclairs, 40-45
    High School Principal, 32-39
    Hog, 18-25
Factory, Shoelace, 54-56
Fingerprints, 48-53
Footprints, Human, 78-83

Graduation Ceremony, 70-77
High School Principal, 32-39
Hog, Prize-Winning, 18-25
Hospital, Animal, 57-61
Human Footprints, 78-83
Principal, High School, 32-39
Prize-Winning Hog, 18-25
Recycling Center, 62-67
Robbery, Recycling Center, 62-67
    Shoelace Factory, 54-56
Strange Occurrences, 68-99
Train, Circus, 26-31

47. On what pages can you read about a robbery? _____

48. Where will you find the Bathtub Ring Case? _____

49. What pages tell about the Shoelace Factory Robbery? _____

50. Where can you read about a strange graduation ceremony? _____

51. Which pages cover strange occurrences? _____

52. Which pages cover burglaries? _____

53. On what pages can you read about disappearances? _____

Use this illustration for questions 54–55.

54. From what the picture shows, which of these statements is probably true? *(Circle the letters.)*

a. The prize puppy is missing.

b. The petnapper climbed over the fence.

c. The petnapping happened in mid-day.

d. The woman called a detective agency.

e. The petnapper climbed into a window.

f. The ladder belongs to the woman.

55. What can you assume from looking at the clothing the woman is wearing? *(Circle the letters.)*

a. The woman usually dresses sloppily.

b. The woman has recently gotten out of bed.

c. The woman hasn't eaten breakfast.

d. All the woman's clothes are at the cleaners.

Name _____

Fifth Grade Book of Language Tests

Use this map for questions 56–60.

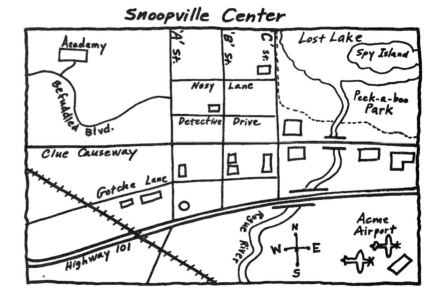

Snoopville Center

56. Which of these does NOT cross Highway 101?
   a. railroad
   b. Rogue River
   c. Clue Causeway
   d. A Street

57. Which is NOT north of Highway 101?
   a. Gottcha Lane
   b. Acme Airport
   c. Nosey Lane
   d. Detective Drive

58. What direction is the Academy from the airport? _____

59. What street lies between Highway 101 and Clue Causeway? _____

60. What direction is Spy Island from B Street? _____

Use this timeline for questions 61–66.

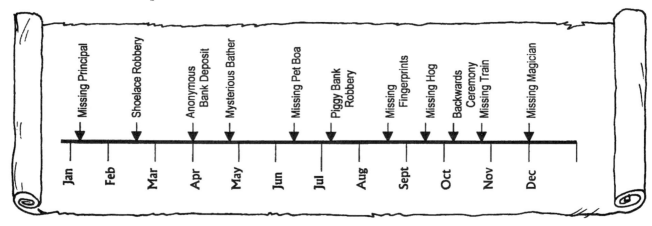

61. About how many months passed between robberies? _____

62. What was missing about 4 months before the train? _____

63. What case took place about 4½ months after the anonymous bank deposit?

_____

64. Which cases took place during the same month?

_____

65. During which months did the detective have no challenging cases?

_____

66. About how many months passed between cases about missing persons? _____

Name _____

Fifth Grade Book of Language Tests

Use this table for questions 67–70.

Super Sleuth Association
Detectives' Areas of Specialty

Detective	Arson	Missing Persons	Tracking	Strange Noises	Missing Pets
Full-Time Detectives	12	18	24	9	12
Part-Time Detectives	7	3	7	0	1
Retired Detectives	2	1	5	0	0

67. What is the total number of part-time detectives? _____

68. What area of specialty has the most retired detectives? _____

69. What area is the least popular with full-time detectives? _____

70. Which group of detectives is most interested in missing pets? _____

Use this graph for questions 71–75.

Case	Time Spent on Case, in Hours
Surf Shop Surveillance	
Internet Caper	
Missing Pet Boa	
Stolen Bagels	
Magician's Disappearance	
Piggy Bank Robbery	

0   10   20   30   40   50   60

71. Which case took about 8 hours?

_____

72. Which case took about 38 hours?

_____

73. How many cases took more time than the Stolen Bagels? _____

74. About how much time was spent on the Piggy Bank Robbery? _____

75. About how much time was spent on the 6 cases total?
   a. about 200 hours
   b. less than 100 hours
   c. about 150 hours
   d. more than 200 hours

Name _____

99

LIBRARY SKILLS

Name _____

Date _____

Possible Correct Answers: 25

Your Correct Answers: _____

1. This book is probably:
   a. fiction
   b. nonfiction
   c. biography

2. This book is probably:
   a. fiction
   b. nonfiction
   c. biography

3. Biographies are organized:
   a. alphabetically by author
   b. alphabetically by title
   c. alphabetically by the person the book is about
   d. in order by publication date

4. Fiction is organized:
   a. alphabetically by author
   b. alphabetically by title
   c. by the Dewey Decimal System
   d. alphabetically by subject

5. If you know the title and subject of a book, but not the author, you could find a book by looking at:
   a. subject card
   b. author card
   c. title card

6. To find a mystery (book) by the author Agatha Christie, which word would you type into the library computer catalog?
   a. Agatha
   b. Christie
   c. mysteries
   d. fiction

Fifth Grade Book of Language Tests   Copyright ©2000 by Incentive Publications, Inc., Nashville, TN.

796
Pe
SPORTS-ANECDOTES
   Fellowski, Michael
Not-So-Great Moments in Sports
   Illust. by Myron Miller
NY: Sterling Pub. Co. © 1994
    95 p. illus.

599.74
Gra
GRAHAM, ADA
   Bears in the Wild
    Illust. by D.D. Tyler
   NY: Dell © 1981
    111 p. illus.

7. What kind of card is this?
   a. author card
   b. subject card
   c. title card

8. Who is the publisher?

_____

9. Is the book illustrated?

_____

10. What is the title?

_____

11. What kind of card is this?
   a. author card
   b. subject card
   c. title card

12. What is the title?

_____

13. What is the copyright date?

_____

14. Who is the illustrator?

_____

15. How many pages are in the book? _____

Use the Dewey Decimal System Guide for questions 16–25. In which section of the library would each of these books be found?
Write the Dewey Decimal System section numbers (for example, write 100–199).

_____ 16. The First Book of Football

_____ 17. Learn to Speak Russian

_____ 18. Poems to Make You Giggle

_____ 19. How to Understand Your Brothers

_____ 20. The Life Story of Herbert D. Livery

_____ 21. Learn Algebra in 10 Easy Lessons

_____ 22. The Race to Outer Space

_____ 23. Chemistry for Kids

_____ 24. Myths of the Sea

_____ 25. Children of Different Cultures

DEWEY DECIMAL SYSTEM
100-199 Philosophy & Psychology
200-299 Religion & Myths
300-399 Social Sciences
400-499 Languages
500-599 Natural Science & Math
600-699 Uses of Science & Technology
700-799 Fine Arts & Sports
800-899 Literature
900-999 History, Geography, Biography

Name

_____

STUDY SKILLS

Name _____　　Possible Correct Answers: 10

Date _____　　Your Correct Answers: _____

CASE # 1

Detective G. Gumshoe received a call at ten o'clock in the morning from the frantic owner of the Olive County Circus. His circus train, carrying all the circus performers, animals, and equipment had disappeared. The circus owner was desperate for help with his problem. The detective grabbed his notebook and pen, and hurried to meet the circus owner.

1. Which of these questions would help the detective learn important information that might help him figure out what happened to the train?
   Circle the letters of the questions that would help solve this mystery.

   A. When did you notice the disappearance?

   B. Who told you about the disappearance?

   C. How long have you owned the circus?

   D. Do you have insurance?

   E. How large was the train?

   F. Who knew the train's schedule?

   G. How many people were on the train?

   H. How old were the animals?

   I. Were all the animals in good health?

   J. What people were on the train?

   K. When was the train last seen?

Case # 2

Detective Snoop expected to attend the wedding of a friend at a large auditorium. Instead of the wedding, he walked into the beginning of a high school graduation ceremony. He was just about to leave when he noticed something peculiar. All the guests were facing the back of the auditorium. The graduates on the stage all had their robes on backwards. One by one, they got up from their seats, walked backwards across the stage, and gave their diplomas back to the principal. As Detective Snoop stood in awe, the graduation ceremony proceeded, with every single event happening backwards.

Skim Case # 2 quickly. Without looking back through the story, answer these questions.

2. What was the first strange thing Detective Snoop noticed?

   _____

   _____

3. Why did Detective Snoop go to the auditorium?

   _____

   _____

4. What did the graduates give to the principal?

   _____

   _____

CASE # 3

"One moment the pig was there. The next moment it was not," explained Mr. P. Razer, who was wearing a straw hat, to Detective B. Sharpe. The detective arrived at noon to hear Mr. Razer's story. The plump, prize-winning pig had been vanishing several times a day, but she always reappeared in her pen. Mr. Razer explained that the pig would be gone for 5-10 minutes at a time. This had happened 12 times in the last 24 hours. Detective Sharpe scratched her head. She looked around. A 5-foot high fence surrounded the pigpen. The gate was securely locked. The weather was turning colder. There were no footprints or pig prints leading away from the pen.

5. What is the main idea of this case?

_____

_____

_____

6. Which details are necessary to know if the case is to be solved?
(Circle all that are necessary.)

A. The pig keeps disappearing.

B. The pig always reappears.

C. Mr. Razer is wearing a hat.

D. The pig is gone 5–10 minutes at a time.

E. The detective arrived at noon.

F. The detective scratches her head.

G. A 5–foot high fence surrounds the pen.

H. The gate is kept locked.

I. The weather is getting colder.

J. There are no footprints.

CASE # 4

At the end of a fabulous dinner, just before the serving of dessert, Chef Henri left the kitchen to take a bow before the guests. When Henri returned to the kitchen, he ordered his helpers to serve the dessert immediately. But something was wrong! All one hundred of his famous chocolate eclairs were missing! "This is impossible!" cried Henri. "No one must leave this building until the desserts are found!" There was not one sign of the eclairs anywhere.

7. Which is the best summary of Case # 4?

a. Chef Henri's dessert eclairs disappeared.

b. Chef Henri was honored at a banquet.

c. Guests were accused of stealing the dessert.

The Case of the Bathtub Ring

I. The House Was Deserted.
  A. No one lived there for 2 months.
  B.
  C. The maid came once a week.
II.
  A. The doors were locked.
  B. There was no sign of entry.
  C. No windows were broken.
  E. There were no footprints outside.
III. The Bathtub Had Been Used.
  A.
  B. Wet footprints were beside the tub.
  C. Two towels were damp.
  D. A wet bar of soap was on the floor.

Write the numbers or letters showing where each of these missing pieces belongs in the outline. (Example: write *III A.*)

8. The Maid Came Last Monday. _____

9. There was a ring around the bathtub. _____

10. The house was always kept locked. _____

Name _____

Fifth Grade Book of Language Tests

Spelling Skills Checklists

Spelling Test # 1:

RULES & RULE-BREAKERS

Test Location: pages 106–107

Skill	*Test Items*
Correctly spell words that use ie rules	1–12
Correctly spell words with double consonants	13–20
Spell words with confusing initial consonant sounds and blends	21–30
Follow rules to spell plurals correctly	31–38
Correctly spell the singular form of a plural noun	39–46
Follow rules to correctly spell different tenses of verbs	47–55
Correctly spell a variety of compound words	56–59
Correctly spell words that break spelling rules	60–70

Spelling Test # 2:

SPELLING WITH WORD PARTS

Test Location: pages 108–109

Skill	*Test Items*
Correctly spell words with prefixes	1–12, 21–24
Correctly spell words with suffixes	13–24, 1, 5, 6, 8–12
Correctly spell words that have a prefix and a suffix	21–24, 1, 5, 8–10
Use knowledge of root spellings to spell words correctly	25–36
Make correct changes to root words when adding *ed, ing,* or *y*	37–43
Distinguish among similar endings; choose the correct ending for accurate spelling	44–70

Fifth Grade Book of Language Tests

Spelling Test # 3:

CONFUSING & TRICKY WORDS

Test Location: pages 110–111

Spelling Test # 4:

CORRECTING SPELLING ERRORS

Test Location: pages 112–116

105

RULES & RULE-BREAKERS

Name _____   Possible Correct Answers: 70

Date _____   Your Correct Answers: _____

Circle the correct spelling for each word.

1. freind friend	4. beleive believe	7. neighbor nieghbor	10. recieve receive
2. weigh wiegh	5. grief greif	8. ceiling cieling	11. receipt reciept
3. cheif chief	6. sleigh sliegh	9. reindeer riendeer	12. veil viel

accident   sylable   Tennesee   tomorrow   glossary

neccesary   diferent   bannannas   misspell

catterpillar   terrible   illegal   alowance   scisors

Find the words that are spelled wrong on Freddy's list. Write them correctly.

13. _____   14. _____   15. _____

16. _____   17. _____   18. _____

19. _____   20. _____

Find the misspelled word in each sentence. Cross out the word, and write it correctly in the space above the sentence.

21. Have you been to the flea sircus?

22. Your hat is all rinkled!

23. Cover your mouth when you kough.

24. The trouble with selery is all the strings.

25. I never saw such a gostly sight!

26. Would you like shugar with that cereal?

27. I have scraped all the skin off my nuckle.

28. Watch out for the kwicksand!

29. Why do you always talk in a wisper?

30. That kid is a jenius!

106

Write each noun in its plural form.

31. tomato _____

32. monkey _____

33. loaf _____

34. mess _____

35. butterfly _____

36. goose _____

37. woman _____

38. country _____

Write the singular form of each noun.

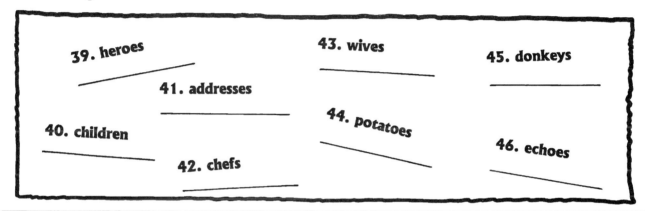

39. heroes _____

41. addresses _____

40. children _____

42. chefs _____

43. wives _____

44. potatoes _____

45. donkeys _____

46. echoes _____

Write each word in its PAST tense.

47. worry _____

48. wish _____

49. argue _____

50. freeze _____

51. forget _____

52. fight _____

53. try _____

54. bring _____

55. think _____

Circle the correctly spelled compound words in each group.

56. hitchhiker   babisitter   firecracker   sholace

57. shipwreck   swimsuit   ponitail   headache

58. countriside   teenager   notbook   nighttime

59. roomate   baseball   firside   bubblgum

These words are all rule-breakers. Choose the correct spelling for each one.

60. weird
    wierd

61. ancient
    anceint

62. hieght
    height

63. pianoes
    pianos

64. noticable
    noticeable

65. truely
    truly

66. niether
    neither

67. wholey
    wholly

68. solos
    soloes

69. pastime
    pasttime

70. foreign
    foriegn

Name _____

Fifth Grade Book of Language Tests

SPELLING WITH WORD PARTS

Name _____   Possible Correct Answers: 70

Date _____   Your Correct Answers: _____

All the words on Francine's test have prefixes or suffixes. Which ones has she spelled correctly?

Find the correct words. Circle their numbers.

Find the incorrect words. Fix the errors by writing the words correctly.

SPELLING TEST

1. extraordinary _____	13. guidence _____
2. recall _____	14. ambulence _____
3. misstake _____	15. completely _____
4. transtport _____	16. possibley _____
5. antebacterial _____	17. appointment _____
6. unhappy _____	18. dentest _____
7. preeview _____	19. acter _____
8. nontoxic _____	20. hopful _____
9. deapartment _____	21. impossibility _____
10. subbmarine _____	22. unadventuresome _____
11. argument _____	23. inconsiderut _____
12. terrific _____	24. irresponsibel _____

Use your knowledge of roots to spell these words correctly. They all have errors.

25. impossibel _____   31. musikal _____

26. biografy _____   32. imperfact _____

27. disapeer _____   33. diference _____

28. advertizement _____   34. frekwently _____

29. axcidental _____   35. faverable _____

30. feeverish _____   36. unsurprizing _____

Fifth Grade Book of Language Tests   Copyright ©2000 by Incentive Publications, Inc., Nashville, TN.

Add *ed*, *y*, or *ing* to the word at the end of each sentence to make it fit correctly. Write the word in the blank in each sentence. Make sure you spell it right!

37. What are you _____ in that strange bundle? **(carry)**

38. There are no fishing licenses _____ here this month. **(require)**

39. "Why are you carrying around that _____ slug?" Tad's dad asked. **(slime)**

40. The kids tried to stop _____ during the concert, but they could not! **(giggle)**

41. When she coughed, the sound _____ through the whole building. **(echo)**

42. "This is the heaviest baboon I have ever _____ !" Tom complained. **(carry)**

43. What a perfect afternoon for a trip to the _____ pool! **(swim)**

It will take more than magic for you to get the correct endings for these words. Circle the ending that will finish the word with the right spelling.

Presto!

44. magic (ian, ion, un, shun)

45. cush (ian, ion, ean, un)

46. vacat (shun, ion, ian, iun)

47. marvel (us, ous, eous)

48. nerv (eous, ous, us, ious)

49. rad (eous, ius, ious)

50. hydr (ent, ant, int)

51. vac (ent, ant, int)

52. sci (ence, ance, ince)

53. insur (ence, ance, anse)

54. ador (ible, eble, able)

55. trav (el, al, il, le)

56. cand (el, al, il, le)

57. icic (el, al, il, le)

58. chocol (at, ate, ite, ete)

59. favor (ate, ete, ite)

60. defin (ate, ete, ite)

61. educat (ate, aet, at, ete)

62. celebr (ate, eat, ete, ite)

63. fool (ish, esh, ash)

64. compl (eat, ete, eet)

65. critic (ise, ize, eize)

66. apolog (ise, ice, ize)

67. garb (ede, age, ige, edge)

68. knowl (ege, age, ige, edge)

69. cour (ege, age, ige, edge)

70. prom (ise, ice, ace)

Fifth Grade Book of Language Tests

CONFUSING & TRICKY WORDS

Name _____

Possible Correct Answers: 45

Date _____

Your Correct Answers: _____

stalk	bridge
ghost	honest
envy	sword
combing	erupt
wriggle	knife

shhhhh

1. Which words on Freddy's poster do NOT have silent letters? Write them below.

_____

_____

_____

If a word is NOT correct, write it correctly on the line beside the incorrectly spelled word.

2. carusel _____

3. mosquitoe _____

4. kindergarden _____

5. spaghetti _____

6. tortila _____

7. waffel _____

8. macaroni _____

9. tornado _____

10. antike _____

11. dinamite _____

Choose the right vowel combination from the chart to spell each word correctly.

12. c _____ ght

13. n _____ sy

14. ag _____ n

15. ann _____ nce

16. str _____ ght

17. thr _____ gh

18. b _____ ty

19. app _____ r

au   ea   oi   eau   ai   ou   ow

20. Look carefully at each of these big words. Circle the words that are spelled incorrectly.

caterpiller	E✹✹XAGGERATE	*circumferance*	multiplacation
encyclopedia	**perpandicular**	percipitation	*orthodontist*
gymnazium	Mississippi	*hippopotamus*	**biodegradable**

21. Circle the correctly-spelled words on Sheriff Frog's poster.

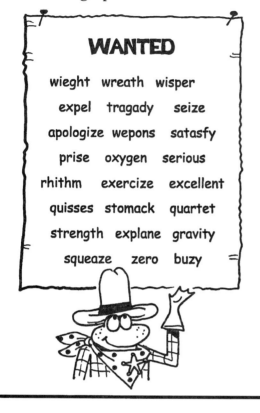

WANTED

wieght   wreath   wisper

expel   tragady   seize

apologize   wepons   satasfy

prise   oxygen   serious

rhithm   exercize   excellent

quisses   stomack   quartet

strength   explane   gravity

squeaze   zero   buzy

Which is the correct spelling for each of these confusing words?

22. a. suprise
    b. surprize
    c. surprise
    d. suprize

23. a. baloon
    b. balloon
    c. ballon
    d. beloon

24. a. marshmellow
    b. marshmallow
    c. marshmelow
    d. marshmalow

25. a. calandar
    b. calender
    c. calendar
    d. callendar

26. bussiness
    b. busness
    c. busniess
    d. business

27. a. necessary
    b. nessessary
    c. necessary
    d. necessary

28. a. embarrass
    b. embarras
    c. embarass
    d. embaras

29. a. abcense
    b. absence
    c. absents
    d. absense

Write the word that correctly finishes each sentence.

30. I heard you were invited to visit the _____ (principle, principal) this morning.

31. That was a frightening _____ (incident, incense) you witnessed today!

32. Did you do a _____ (through, though, thorough) job of cleaning?

33. This is not a family restaurant; we do not serve _____ (miners, minors).

34. Will you be having bananas flambé for _____ (desert, dessert)?

35. My library book has been _____ (overdue, overdo) for a week.

36. Of course I'm not _____ (sacred, scared) of the sea monster.

37. My cat actually _____ (pried, pride) open the cat food box!

38. My _____ (hoarse, horse) is too old to ride anymore.

39. Count the _____ (angels, angles) in your rectangle.

40. I write in my _____ (dairy, diary) every day.

41. What a(n) _____ (perspiring, inspiring) story!

42. Do you like the _____ (salary, celery) in your salad?

43. I _____ (except, accept) your apology.

44. _____ (Adopt, Adept) a pet today!

45. Don't _____ (break, brake) any bones.

Name _____

111

CORRECTING SPELLING ERRORS

Name _____   Possible Correct Answers: 80

Date _____   Your Correct Answers: _____

Choose the correctly-spelled proper noun in each group.

1. **Atlantic, Antartica, Pacifick**
2. **Lincon, Warshington, Jupiter**
3. **Checago, Michigan, Las Angelas**
4. **Wednesday, Tuseday, Saterday**
5. **Chrissmas, Haloween, Thanksgiving**
6. **Brasil, Eqypt, australia, Rushia**
7. **Michigen, Illinois, Oregone, Ioway**
8. **Colarado, Calafornia, Flordia, Maine**

Are these words spelled correctly?
Write *yes* or *no* next to each word.

_____ 9. tommorrow

_____ 10. Tennessee

_____ 11. memmory

_____ 12. bannana

_____ 13. terrible

_____ 14. annimal

_____ 15. syllable

_____ 16. carnivle

Circle the correct spelling of each word.

17. labratory	19. license	21. resturant	23. chocolate
laberatory	lisense	restraunt	chocolat
laboratory	lisence	resterant	chocalat
labretory	licence	restaurant	chocalate
18. twelth	20. vagatable	22. memarise	24. trubble
twelvth	vegetable	memorise	troubble
twelveth	vejetable	memorize	truble
twelfth	veggetable	memmorize	trouble

25. Which words on the chef's shopping list are spelled WRONG? Write them correctly below.

SHOPPING LIST

vegtables
custard
suger
macaroni
spaghetti
chocolate
lettuse
onions
sausage
tomatos
noodels

_____
_____
_____
_____

These words are all misspelled. Write them correctly.

26. pilat _____

27. peopel _____

28. cought _____

29. molacule _____

30. lama _____

31. lafter _____

32. agin _____

33. appeer _____

34. enugh _____

Which word is spelled correctly?
Circle the correct spelling.

35. separate, seperate

36. absence, abcense

37. criticize, criticise

38. wheather, weather

39. autamatic, automatic

40. license, lisence

Circle the word in each group that is NOT spelled correctly.

41. tomatoes
    torpedoes
    pianoes
    volcanoes
    solos

42. wierd
    ancient
    their
    height
    beige

43. homework
    bookkeeper
    roommate
    notbook
    somebody

44. completely
    magecal
    favorable
    accidental
    dentist

45. subbmarine
    transport
    exclude
    semicircle
    antiwar

46. terrifick
    agreement
    dangerous
    explosion
    tropical

47. arithmatic
    caterpillar
    elegant
    Pennsylvania
    hippopotamus

48. galaxy
    astronot
    comical
    rotation
    atmosphere

Name _____

Fifth Grade Book of Language Tests

Which words on Pierre's poster are NOT
correct? Write them on the lines correctly.

49. _____

50. _____

51. _____

52. _____

53. _____

54. _____

firecracker   celery   enerjy

couffed   surprice   phone

skuba   sider   babisitter

In each sentence below, find a word that is misspelled.
Write it correctly on the line before the sentence.

_____ 55. Don't get your tounge twisted when you practice those riddles.

_____ 56. Is that a mosquitoe buzzing around your tomato?

_____ 57. What an offensive oder is coming from the restaurant's kitchen!

_____ 58. Every time I have a fantastic idea, Freddy's idea is oppisite.

Fix the tough words on Francie's list. She has misspelled them all. Write them correctly.

59. kechup _____   64. Saterday _____

60. spinetch _____   65. allmost _____

61. lonliness _____   66. becuz _____

62. tangel _____   67. twoard _____

63. advertize _____   68. emty _____

Write the message on each sign again, spelling all the words correctly.
Use the lines beneath the signs.

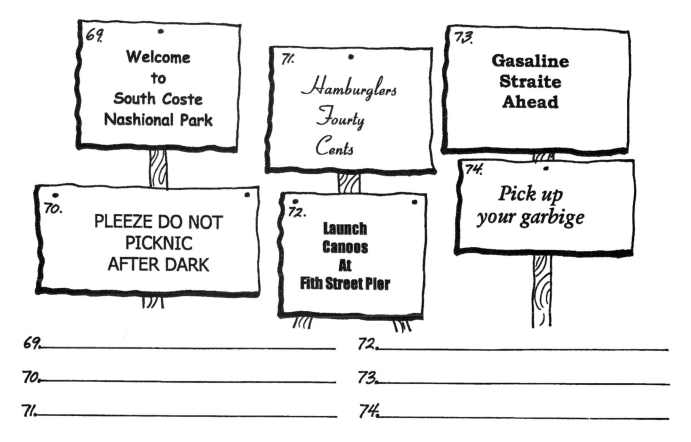

69. _____

70. _____

71. _____

72. _____

73. _____

74. _____

75. Correct the spelling of this letter. Cross out any misspelled words; write each correctly above the word it replaces.

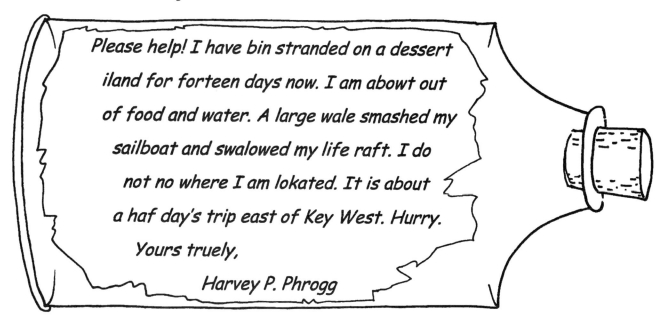

Rewrite each headline, spelling all the words correctly.

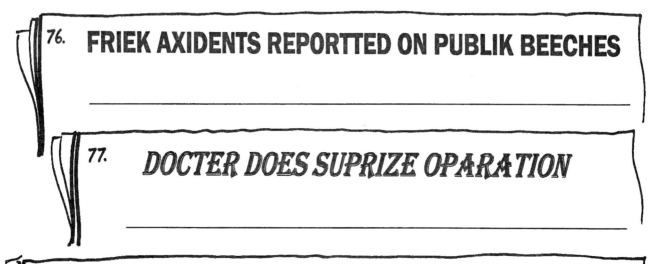

76. FRIEK AXIDENTS REPORTTED ON PUBLIK BEECHES

_____

77. DOCTER DOES SUPRIZE OPARATION

_____

78. SKI SESON CANCELLED DUE TO DANGROUS ICE STORM

_____

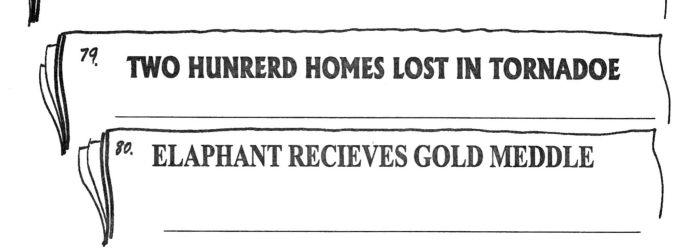

79. TWO HUNRERD HOMES LOST IN TORNADOE

_____

80. ELAPHANT RECIEVES GOLD MEDDLE

_____

KEEPING TRACK OF SKILLS

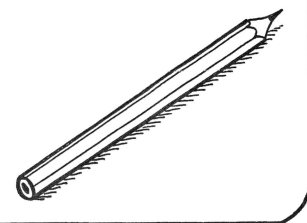

STUDENT PROGRESS RECORD — LANGUAGE SKILLS

Student Name _____

TEST DATE	READING TESTS	SCORE	COMMENTS & NEEDS
	Test # 1 Word Meanings	of 70	
	Test # 2 Literal Comprehension	of 40	
	Test # 3 Inferential & Evaluative Comprehension	of 35	
	Test # 4 Literature	of 55	

TEST DATE	WRITING TESTS	SCORE	COMMENTS & NEEDS
	Test # 1 Word Choice & Word Use	of 25	
	Test # 2 Forms & Techniques	of 35	
	Test # 3 Content & Organization	of 50	
	Test # 4 Editing	of 50	
	Test # 5 Writing Process	of 30	

TEST DATE	GRAMMAR & USAGE TESTS	SCORE	COMMENTS & NEEDS
	Test # 1 Parts of Speech	of 80	
	Test # 2 Sentences	of 30	
	Test # 3 Capitalization & Punctuation	of 50	
	Test # 4 Language Usage	of 70	

TEST DATE	WORDS & VOCABULARY SKILLS TESTS	SCORE	COMMENTS & NEEDS
	Test # 1 Word Parts	of 70	
	Test # 2 Vocabulary Word Meanings	of 45	
	Test # 3 Confusing Words	of 75	

TEST DATE	STUDY & RESEARCH SKILLS TESTS	SCORE	COMMENTS & NEEDS
	Test # 1 Dictionary & Encyclopedia Skills	of 50	
	Test # 2 Reference & Information Skills	of 75	
	Test # 3 Library Skills	of 25	
	Test # 4 Study Skills	of 10	

TEST DATE	SPELLING TESTS	SCORE	COMMENTS & NEEDS
	Test # 1 Rules & Rule-Breakers	of 70	
	Test # 2 Spelling with Word Parts	of 70	
	Test # 3 Confusing & Tricky Words	of 45	
	Test # 4 Correcting Spelling Errors	of 80	

Fifth Grade Book of Language Tests

CLASS PROGRESS RECORD – LANGUAGE SKILLS
(Reading, Writing, Grammar & Usage)

Class _____

Teacher _____

READING TESTS

TEST DATE	TEST	COMMENTS ABOUT RESULTS	SKILLS NEEDING RE-TEACHING
	Test # 1 Word Meanings		
	Test # 2 Literal Comprehension		
	Test # 3 Inferential & Evaluative Comprehension		
	Test # 4 Literature Skills		

WRITING TESTS

TEST DATE	TEST	COMMENTS ABOUT RESULTS	SKILLS NEEDING RE-TEACHING
	Test # 1 Word Choice & Word Use		
	Test # 2 Forms & Techniques		
	Test # 3 Content & Organization		
	Test # 4 Editing		
	Test # 5 Writing Process		

GRAMMAR & USAGE TESTS

TEST DATE	TEST	COMMENTS ABOUT RESULTS	SKILLS NEEDING RE-TEACHING
	Test # 1 Parts of Speech		
	Test # 2 Sentences		
	Test # 3 Capitalization & Punctuation		
	Test # 4 Language Usage		

CLASS PROGRESS RECORD — LANGUAGE SKILLS

(Words & Vocabulary Skills, Study & Research Skills, Spelling)

Class _____   Teacher _____

WORDS & VOCABULARY SKILLS TESTS

TEST DATE	TEST	COMMENTS ABOUT RESULTS	SKILLS NEEDING RE-TEACHING
	Test # 1 Word Parts		
	Test # 2 Vocabulary Word Meanings		
	Test # 3 Confusing Words		

STUDY & RESEARCH SKILLS TESTS

TEST DATE	TEST	COMMENTS ABOUT RESULTS	SKILLS NEEDING RE-TEACHING
	Test # 1 Dictionary & Encyclopedia Skills		
	Test # 2 Reference & Information Skills		
	Test # 3 Library Skills		
	Test # 4 Study Skills		

SPELLING TESTS

TEST DATE	TEST	COMMENTS ABOUT RESULTS	SKILLS NEEDING RE-TEACHING
	Test # 1 Rules & Rule-Breakers		
	Test # 2 Spelling with Word Parts		
	Test # 3 Confusing & Tricky Words		
	Test # 4 Correcting Spelling Errors		

Fifth Grade Book of Language Tests

GOOD SKILL SHARPENERS
FOR LANGUAGE ARTS

The tests in this book will identify student needs for practice, re-teaching or reinforcement of basic skills.

Once those areas of need are known, then what? You and your students need to find some good ways to strengthen those skills.

The BASIC/Not Boring Skills Series, published by Incentive Publications (www.incentivepublications.com), offers fourteen books to sharpen basic skills at the Grades 4–5 level. Six of these books are full of language exercises in the areas of reading, writing, grammar and language usage, study and research, vocabulary and word skills, and spelling.

The pages of these books are student-friendly, clever, and challenging—guaranteed not to be boring! They cover a wide range of skills, including the skills assessed in this book of tests. A complete checklist of skills is available at the front of each book, complete with a reference list directing you to the precise pages for polishing those skills.

TEST IN THIS BOOK **Fifth Grade Book of Language Tests**	Pages in this Book	You will find pages to sharpen skills in these locations from the BASIC/Not Boring Skills Series, published by Incentive Publications.
Reading Test # 1 **Word Meanings**	12–17	Gr. 4–5 Reading Comprehension Gr. 4–5 Words & Vocabulary
Reading Test # 2 **Literal Comprehension**	18–23	Gr. 4–5 Reading Comprehension Gr. 4–5 Study & Research
Reading Test # 3 **Inferential & Evaluative Comprehension**	24–29	Gr. 4–5 Reading Comprehension Gr. 4–5 Study & Research
Reading Test # 4 **Literature Skills**	30–35	Gr. 4–5 Reading Comprehension
Writing Test # 1 **Word Choice & Word Use**	38–39	Gr. 4–5 Writing
Writing Test # 2 **Forms & Techniques**	40–43	Gr. 4–5 Writing
Writing Test # 3 **Content & Organization**	44–47	Gr. 4–5 Writing
Writing Test # 4 **Editing**	48–51	Gr. 4–5 Writing Gr. 4–5 Grammar & Usage
Writing Test # 5 **Writing Process**	52–59	Gr. 4–5 Writing

(continued on next page)

Fifth Grade Book of Language Tests

TEST IN THIS BOOK 5th Grade Book of Language Tests	Pages in this Book	You will find pages to sharpen skills in these locations from the BASIC/Not Boring Skills Series, published by Incentive Publications.
Grammar & Usage Test # 1 **Parts of Speech**	62–65	Gr. 4–5 Grammar & Usage
Grammar & Usage Test # 2 **Sentences**	66–67	Gr. 4–5 Grammar & Usage
Grammar & Usage Test # 3 **Capitalization & Punctuation**	68–71	Gr. 4–5 Grammar & Usage Gr. 4–5 Writing
Grammar & Usage Test # 4 **Language Usage**	72–75	Gr. 4–5 Grammar & Usage
Words & Vocabulary Skills Test # 1 **Word Parts**	78–79	Gr. 4–5 Words & Vocabulary Gr. 4–5 Spelling
Words & Vocabulary Skills Test # 2 **Vocabulary Word Meanings**	80–83	Gr. 4–5 Words & Vocabulary Gr. 4–5 Reading Comprehension
Words & Vocabulary Skills Test # 3 **Confusing Words**	84–87	Gr. 4–5 Words & Vocabulary Gr. 4–5 Spelling
Study & Research Skills Test # 1 **Dictionary & Encyclopedia Skills**	90–93	Gr. 4–5 Study & Research
Study & Research Skills Test # 2 **Reference & Information Skills**	94–99	Gr. 4–5 Study & Research Gr. 4–5 Reading Comprehension
Study & Research Skills Test # 3 **Library Skills**	100–101	Gr. 4–5 Study & Research
Study & Research Skills Test # 4 **Study Skills**	102–103	Gr. 4–5 Study & Research
Spelling Test # 1 **Rules & Rule-Breakers**	106–107	Gr. 4–5 Spelling
Spelling Test # 2 **Spelling with Word Parts**	108–109	Gr. 4–5 Spelling
Spelling Test # 3 **Confusing & Tricky Words**	110–111	Gr. 4–5 Spelling
Spelling Test # 4 **Correcting Spelling Errors**	112–116	Gr. 4–5 Spelling Gr. 4–5 Writing

SCORING GUIDES & ANSWER KEYS

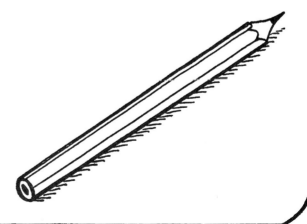

READING TESTS ANSWER KEY

Word Meanings (Test on page 12)

1. a	36. a
2. c	37. d
3. c	38. d
4. b	39. c
5. d	40. suspend, depend
6. d	41. dormant, dormitory
7. c	42. manual, manufacture
8. c	43. laboratory
9. b	44. transfer, ferry
10. a	45. visible, video
11. a	46. mobility
12. b	47. biography
13. d	48. sonic, telephone
14. c	49. thermometer
15. menacing	50. C
16. scrutinize	51. D
17. colossal	52. B
18. perils	53. A
19. probe	54. B or C
20. precarious or treacherous	55. D
21. valiant	56. C or B
22. ultimate	57. A
23. bizarre	58. I
24. primitive	59. P
25. a	60. B
26. d	61. K
27. b	62. A
28. b	63. F
29. c	64. D
30. b	65. G
31. a	66. M
32. a	67. C
33. a	68. N
34. d	69. O
35. c	70. H

Fifth Grade Book of Language Tests

READING TESTS ANSWER KEY

Literal Comprehension (Test on page 18)

1. c
2. a
3. a
4. B
5. 8, 9
6. 4, 5, 6
7. a
8. c
9. b
10. a
11. A and D
12. B, C, and G
13. speed-skiing record
14. blizzard
15. June 5
16. d
17. 4, 5, 2, 3, 1
18. 3
19. Knighthood Revisited
20. The Adventure Store or Decked Out Company
21. Decked Out Company
22. The Adventure Store
23. yes
24. $120
25. The Adventure Store, Little Egypt
26. natron
27. 230 feet
28. 1
29. Dan and Al
30. 110 feet
31. no
32. Check student drawings to see that they show completed drawing of bicycle.
33. 250–263
34. Biking (BMX)
35. 3
36. 20–25
37. 28–29, 32–33, 228–249
38. no
39. Land Sports
40. in the section on B.A.S.E. jumping (160–171) or the glossary (p 282)

READING TESTS ANSWER KEY

Inferential & Evaluative Comprehension (Test on page 24)

1. b
2. d
3. c & d
4. d
5. a
6. b
7. a
8. d
9. b
10. a
11. b
12. F
13. F
14. F
15. O
16. C
17. E
18. E
19. C
20. yes
21. no
22. yes
23. yes
24. a
25. c
26. a, b, d, e
27. e
28. a
29. yes
30. no
31. no
32. no
33. yes
34. yes
35. no

Fifth Grade Book of Language Tests

READING TESTS ANSWER KEY

Literature Skills (Test on page 30)

1. Answers may vary: The balcony of a dwelling at night *or* Outside a dwelling of some sort (at night).
2. the mysterious figure on the balcony
3. the watcher in the bushes
4. c (b is an option)
5. d
6. c
7. b
8. poem
9. c
10. b
11. Answers may vary; accept any two of these:
    - shrieked in horror
    - trembled and shook with dread
    - cried like a baby
    - stopped breathing like the dead
    - sheer terror
    - shuddered till I grew pale
12. fierce, chasing, monstrous, grotesque, mighty, deadly, shuddered (any of these are correct)
13. Accept any three or more of these: massive, rising, grasping, writhing, serpent
14. yes
15. sounds or things heard
16. crossing senses: ability to hear something that is not a sound
17. begins every line with "I hear"
18. b, d, and e
19. a, b, c, d, e, and f
20. d
21. A
22. RT and/or RP
23. RP and/or RT
24. S
25. H
26. S

27. H
28. M
29. P
30. PN
31. A
32. I
33. P
34. P
35. PN
36. S
37. PN
38. R, RT, and/or O
39. R
40. P
41. *e* and *f* are not used and should be circled. Students may or may not decide that *c* and/or *g* are used. Allow these answers either as circled or uncircled.
42. 7
43. b
44. school lunches
45. Students will probably choose one of these:
    - congealed chicken supreme
    - slimy orange carrots in cream,
    - surfing the sky
    - keeps another in his drawer
    - a spot in the town's ambulance
46. c
47. a
48. play
49. joke
50. autobiography
51. dialogue
52. letter
53. advertisement
54. news report
55. recipe

WRITING TESTS ANSWER KEY

Word Choice & Word Use (Test on page 38)

1. b
2. b
3. e
4. d
5. c
6. b
7. a
8. b
9. a, c, d
10. B, C, E, F

11–13. Answers may vary somewhat. Allow any answer that is similar to the following:

11. hurried or rushed mood
12. silly or fun mood
13. secretive or mysterious mood
14. c
15. b
16. a
17. circled
18. circled
19. not circled
20. circled
21. circled
22. circled
23. not circled
24. circled
25. circled

Forms & Techniques (Test on page 40)

1. smell
2. feeling
3. hearing
4. sight
5. A
6. On Sunday evening, Grady came to my house. I showed him my box of truffles. While he was in my room, I got a phone call and went downstairs. The next morning, I found that every truffle had a hole in it. Someone had eaten the middle of each one! Oliver explained that Grady had been the only one in his room all evening. I am deathly allergic to chocolate. (No, your honor is optional.)
7. P or D
8. EX
9. IM
10. EX or P
11. IM
12. P
13. b
14. c
15. parents and teachers (or adults)
16. kids
17. E
18. P
19. R
20. S
21. S
22. P or E
23. M
24. S
25. A
26. P
27. I or E
28. S
29. poem
30. joke
31. news article
32. biography or story
33. advertisement
34. news editorial or essay
35. letter or speech

Fifth Grade Book of Language Tests

WRITING TESTS ANSWER KEY

Content & Organization (Test on page 44)

To the adult:
The ten writing tasks will have varied answers. Assign 1–5 points for each, depending upon how well the student followed the directions, and how thoroughly the work is done. Do not emphasize spelling, punctuation, and capitalization too much in scoring, as it will obscure attention to the skills being examined in each task.

Answers are given below only for those tasks that clearly have right answers:

Task # 3
7, 4, 3, 5, 6, 2, 1 OR 7, 4, 3, 5, 6, 1, 2
   (Students may argue for a
   different sequence.)

Editing (Test on page 48)

To the adult:
   Many of the ten editing tasks will have varied answers. Assign 1–5 points for each, depending upon how well the student followed the directions, and how thoroughly the work is done. Do not emphasize spelling, punctuation, and capitalization too much in scoring, except for in Task # 10, as it will obscure attention to the skills being examined in each task.

   Answers are given below only for those tasks that clearly have correct answers:

Task # 3
   1. Cross out *In my opinion* or *I think.*
      Cross out *even a bit*
   2. Cross out *totally* or *whole.*
   3. Cross out *3-sided.*
   4. Cross out *In addition* or *as well.*

Task # 4
Left side: Cross out:
   I am an out-of-town visitor
   from Memphis.
   The restaurant advertises on TV.
   By the way, my name is Joe.
Right side: Cross out:
   A few more restaurants would be a
   good idea, too.
   And the town needs a better park.

Task # 5
   Left side: 4, 2, 3, 5, 1
   Right side: 3, 5, 1, 4, 2

Task # 10
Phrases and words that are repetitive and should be crossed out.
   * Either: which the city built or owned
      by the city
   * to come
   * It is good for kids, but you are keeping
      them away. OR This is a wonderful
      activity for kids.

Fifth Grade Book of Language Tests

WRITING PROCESS SCORING GUIDE

TRAIT	SCORE OF 5	SCORE OF 3	SCORE OF 1
CONTENT	• The writing is very clear and focused. • The main ideas and purpose stand out clearly. • Main ideas are well-supported with details and examples. • All details are relevant to the main idea. • The ideas have some freshness and insight. • The ideas fit the purpose and audience well. • The paper is interesting and holds the reader's attention.	• The writing is mostly clear and focused. • The main ideas and purpose are mostly clear. • Details and examples are used but may be somewhat limited or repetitive. • Most details are relevant to the main idea. • Some details may be off the topic. • Some ideas and details are fresh; others are ordinary. • The paper is interesting to some degree. • The ideas and content are less than precisely right for the audience and purpose.	• The writing lacks clarity and focus. • It is hard to identify the main idea. • The purpose of the writing is not evident. • Details are few, not relevant, or repetitive. • Ideas or details have little sparkle or appeal to hold the reader's attention. • The paper has not developed an idea well.
WORD CHOICE	• Writer has used strong, specific, colorful, effective, and varied words. • Words are used well to convey the ideas. • Words are well chosen to fit the content, audience, and purpose. • Writer has chosen fresh, unusual words, and/or has used words/phrases in an unusual way. • Writer has made use of figurative language, and words/phrases that create images.	• Writer has used some specific and effective words. • A good use of colorful, unusual words is attempted, but limited or overdone. • The words succeed at conveying main ideas. • The writer uses words in fresh ways sometimes, but not consistently. • The word choice is mostly suited to the content, audience, and purpose.	• There is a limited use of specific, effective, or colorful words. • Some words chosen are imprecise, misused, or repetitive. • The words do not suit the content, purpose, or audience well. • The words do not succeed at conveying the main ideas.
SENTENCES	• Sentences have a pleasing and natural flow. • When read aloud, sentences and ideas flow along smoothly from one to another. • Transitions between sentences are smooth and natural. • Sentences have varied length, structure, sound, and rhythm. • The structure of sentences focuses reader's attention on the main idea and key details. • The sentence sound and variety make the reading enjoyable. • If the writer uses dialogue, it is used correctly and effectively.	• Most of the sentences have a natural flow. • When read aloud, some sentences have a "less than fluid" sound. • Some or all transitions are awkward or repetitive. • There is some variety in sentence length, structure, sound, and rhythm; but some patterns are repetitive. • The sentences convey the main idea and details, but without much craftsmanship. • If the writer uses dialogue, it is somewhat less than fluid or effective.	• Most sentences are not fluid. • When read aloud, the writing sounds awkward or uneven. Some of the paper is confusing to read. • Transitions are not effective. • There is little variety in sentence length, structure, sound, or rhythm. • There may be incomplete or run-on sentences. • The sentence structure gets in the way of conveying content, purpose, and meaning.

A score of 4 may be given for papers that fall between 3 and 5 on a trait. A score of 2 may be given for papers that fall between 1 and 3.

WRITING PROCESS SCORING GUIDE

TRAIT	SCORE OF 5	SCORE OF 3	SCORE OF 1
ORGANIZATION	• The organization of the piece allows the main ideas and key details to be conveyed well. • The piece has a compelling beginning that catches the attention of the reader. • Ideas are developed in a clear, interesting sequence. • The piece moves along from one idea, sentence, or paragraph to another in a manner that is smooth and useful to develop the meaning. • The piece has a compelling ending that ties up the idea well and leaves the reader feeling pleased.	• Organization is recognizable, but weak or inconsistent in some places. • For the most part, the organization of the piece allows the main ideas and key details to be conveyed. • The structure seems somewhat ordinary, lacking flavor or originality. • The piece has a beginning that is not particularly inviting to the reader or not well-developed. • Some of the sequencing is confusing. • The piece does not always move along smoothly or clearly from one idea, sentence, or paragraph to another. • The piece has clear ending, but it is somewhat dull or underdeveloped, or does not adequately tie up the piece.	• The piece lacks clear organization. • For the most part, the lack of good organization gets in the way of the conveyance of the main ideas and key details. • The piece does not have a clear beginning or ending. • Ideas are not developed in any clear sequence, or the sequence is distracting. • The piece does not move along smoothly from one sentence or paragraph to another. • Important ideas or details seem to be missing or out of place. • The piece leaves the reader feeling confused.
VOICE	• The writer has left a personal stamp on the piece. A reader knows there is a person behind the writing. • It is clear that the writer knows what audience and purpose he/she is reaching. • The writer engages the audience. • The writer shows passion, commitment, originality, and honesty in conveying the message. • The voice used (level of personal closeness) is appropriate for the purpose of the piece.	• The writer has left a personal stamp on the piece, but this is not as strong or consistent as it might be. The reader is not always sure of the writer's presence. • It is not always clear that the writer knows his/her audience and purpose. • The writer engages the audience some, but not all of the time. • The writer shows some passion, commitment, originality, and honesty in conveying the message, but this is inconsistent.	• The writer has not left any personal stamp on the piece. The writing feels detached. • There is little sense that the writer is speaking to the audience or clearly knows the purpose of the writing. • There is little or no engagement of the audience. • The writer shows little or no passion, commitment, originality, and honesty in conveying the message.
CONVENTIONS	• There is clear control of capitalization, punctuation, spelling, and paragraphing. • There is consistent use of correct grammar and language usage. • The strong use of conventions strengthens the communication of the work's meaning. • The piece needs little editing/revision.	• There is some control of capitalization, punctuation, spelling, and paragraphing. • There is inconsistent use of correct grammar and language usage. • The uneven use of conventions sometimes interferes with the meaning. • The piece needs much editing/revision.	• There is poor control of capitalization, punctuation, spelling, and paragraphing. • There is a lack of correct grammar and language usage. • Poor use of conventions obscures meaning. • There are multiple errors; the piece needs extensive editing/revision.

A score of 4 may be given for papers that fall between 3 and 5 on a trait. A score of 2 may be given for papers that fall between 1 and 3.

131

GRAMMAR & USAGE TESTS ANSWER KEY

Parts of Speech (Test on page 62)

1. AJ
2. V
3. AJ
4. N
5. N
6. AD
7. AJ
8. N
9. V
10. AD
11. AD
12. N
13. story, campers (optional Freddy's)
14. frightened
15. Freddy's, ghost, oldest
16. adjective
17. adjective
18. spiders, beds, moss, stew
19. Friday, Billy
20. our
21. compasses
22. knives
23. tomatoes
24. deer
25. families
26. bushes
27. mouse

28. child
29. city
30. goose
31. woman
32. brother-in-law
33. foxes' teeth
34. mouse's chocolate
35. 3 campers' shirts
36. fox's teeth
37. frog's legs
38. skunk's tail
39. counselors' tent
40. goose's honk
41. children's screams
42. waterfall's roar
43. They
44. This or she
45. We
46. us
47. them
48. rowed
49. will swim, or swam, or is swimming
50. fell or has fallen
51. flies, will fly, or will be flying
52. wore

53. wrote, have written, or will write
54. fainted
55. voted
56. tell
57. think
58. Are
59. find
60. stop
61. eat
62. see
63. screamed
64. wiggled
65. crept or stayed
66. imagine
67. is
68. should
69. should or be or should be
70. is or have or were
71. adjective or noun
72. adverb
73. adjective
74. noun
75. verb
76. adjective
77. adverb
78. B, A
79. B, A
80. B, A

Fifth Grade Book of Language Tests

GRAMMAR & USAGE TESTS ANSWER KEY

Sentences (Test on page 66)

1. F
2. R
3. C
4. C
5. F
6. CD
7. CX
8. S
9. CX
10. S
11. F
12. A, C, E
13. G, H
14. B, D
15. Sam
16. bears
17. chipmunk
18. crashed
19. catch
20. watched

21–24. Answers may vary somewhat from those shown below. Make sure student has written the sentences so that the modifying phrases are accurately placed and the sentence makes sense.

21. A fish jumped up and bit me while I was rowing in a rowboat.
22. I read in a magazine about a counselor who taught scuba diving.
23. I saw a large snake hanging from a limb.
24. While the horses were eating hay, I looked them over and decided which one to ride.
25. the tired swimmers
26. the three hungry campers
27. Counselors and campers
28. have never before seen so many cockroaches in one place
29. chased them under the bunks and across the floor
30. hang from the corners of our cabin

GRAMMAR & USAGE TESTS ANSWER KEY

Capitalization & Punctuation (Test on page 68)

1. Monday, July, 14
   Dear Mom and Dad,
   I love being at Camp Lookout. You wouldn't believe what fun I'm having. One of my bunk-mates is from Australia, and the other one is from the British West Indies. I ate four hot dogs, seven doughboys, and six s'mores on our campout! Do you believe that? Also, I have had poison ivy all week, and I got a snake bite. I love this place! I have a pet dragonfly. Could you please send me more money for the snack bar?
   Love,
   Maria
2. Circle: On, July, Oregon, Camp, Lookout, Pacific, Ocean
3. Circle: The, Europe, French, Saturday.
4. a
5. 100 Different Ways to Toast a Marshmallow
6. Encyclopedia of Camps in the United States
7. How to Track a Sasquatch
8. circled—okay
9. Stories to Tell Around the Campfire
10. circled—okay
11. will not
12. she will
13. he would
14. were not
15. I have
16. couldn't
17. we've
18. they're
19. we'd
20. aren't
21. b
22. d
23. Circle: A, D, H, I
24. "Is it true," asked Flo, "that you ran into a bear on your hike this morning?"
25. Janice wondered, "Jim, how many marshmallows did you really eat last night?"
26. "I never should have packed this many clothes," Tara complained, as she did her laundry.
27. At the campfire, Counselor Carla said, "I notice that Frankie is not here tonight."
28. "You're not the only camper who's dreading survival training," said Michael.
29. "The food at Camp Lookout," bragged the cook, "is the best in the whole country."
30. "But I've never sailed a boat before!" wailed Todd as the wind pushed the boat around.
31. "We don't really believe your story about the fish," Jessica's friends told her.
32. The camp director announced, "There is a big storm coming and we must get ready."
33–41. *(A period at the end of each sentence is optional.)*
33. Mt. Ivy is straight ahead.
34. You are two miles from Adams Lake.
35. Caution! The trail to Grizzly Peak is covered with patches of ice.
36. Do not feed the animals or pick the wild flowers.
37. Horses must use Green Lake Trail.
38. Follow Sunrise Trail west to Button Butte.
39. Stay on the trail!
40. No glass is allowed on the trail. (or !)
41. There is a $1000 fine for littering.

Fifth Grade Book of Language Tests

GRAMMAR & USAGE TESTS ANSWER KEY

Language Usage (Test on page 72)

1. have
2. are
3. have
4. has
5. were
6. spend
7. raise
8. teach
9. guides
10. make
11. their
12. it
13. them
14. c
15. a
16. b
17. a
18. them
19. me
20. We
21. her
22. I
23. b
24. d
25. C, E, and H are correct
26. hoarse
27. there
28. meet
29. their
30. Your, hole
31. been, see

32–47: Corrected form should look like this:

32. The weather looks good today.
33. Congratulations! You all did well on the midnight hike
34. Today our campers showed that they can all swim well!
35. Who missed J.J.'s scary stories? You would have loved them!
36. Don't leave your sleeping bags out in the rain.
37. Everyone should have come with us to the tar pits!
38. We'll let everyone sleep in on Saturday morning.
39. I can teach anyone how to yodel.
40. Don't sit too close to the edge of the bluff.
41. May I borrow someone's compass?
42. Don't set your sleeping bag too close to the fire.
43. I'm looking for someone to sit with me at the rodeo.
44. It's good that you're all here at Camp Lookout!
45. Isn't it amazing how Jamie got away from that bear?
46. Doesn't everyone feel good about the talent show?
47. The comet will appear about midnight.
48. faster
49. farthest
50. slimiest
51. earlier
52. most often
53. more strangely
54. better
55. less
56. worst
57. under
58. from
59. into
60. across
61. without a life jacket
62. During the night
63. beneath your bed
64. above your head
65. outside the door
66. worms
67. towels
68. pranks
69. commotion
70. night

Fifth Grade Book of Language Tests

WORDS & VOCABULARY SKILLS TESTS ANSWER KEY

Word Parts (Test on page 78)

1. preview
2. miniature
3. antibiotic
4. centipede
5. mistake
6. transport
7. uniform
8. improper
9. submerge
10. ashore
11. regain
12. semicircle
13. expel
14. octagon
15. supervisor
16. bicycle
17. cooperate
18. postwar
19. misread
20. disapprove
21. exhale
22. inconsistent
23. microchip
24. midfield
25. nonstop
26. superhuman
27. unicycle
28. pentagon
29. malfunction
30. transatlantic
31. rewrite
32. co-write
33. semi-complete
34. antifreeze
35. actor
36. terrify

37. hopeful
38. friendless
39. piglets
40. wooden
41. homeward
42. loneliness
43. perilous
44. stormy
45. hopeless
46. troublesome
47. backwards
48. sailor
49. silken
50. droplets
51. cowardly
52. friendship
53. I
54. L
55. A
56. O
57. M
58. B
59. F
60. J
61. N
62. C
63. E
64. K
65. H
66. G
67. D
68. waterfall, seaside
69. candlestick, seasick, shipwreck, sunstroke
70. fireside, swimsuit, surfboard

Fifth Grade Book of Language Tests

WORDS & VOCABULARY SKILLS TESTS ANSWER KEY

Vocabulary Word Meanings (Test on page 80)

1. flotsam
2. a mariner
3. a borscht
4. a vicar
5. yes
6. enemy
7. cordial
8. chide
9. morose
10. villain
11. prevaricate
12. famished
13. maelstrom
14. aroma
15. punctual
16. c
17. d
18. a
19. b
20. a
21. rude
22. flimsy
23. cautious
24. slowed

25. permanent
26. Answers may vary somewhat: odd, strange
27. Answers may vary somewhat: able to do things well with both hands
28. c
29. b
30. snatched
31. absence
32. crude
33. terrified
34. calm
35. proceed
36. tender
37. tranquil
38. b
39. b
40. shipwreck
41. sunburn
42. fire
43. track
44. spot
45. coast

Fifth Grade Book of Language Tests

Confusing Words (Test on page 84)

1. buried
2. heard
3. threw
4. towed
5. straight
6. caught
7. clothes
8. groan
9. taught
10. need
11. know or aloud
12. ate
13. hire or weak or serf
14. rode or peer
15. mane or main
16. sees, seize, or hi
17. knot
18. sales or hear
19. beech
20. meteorite
21. effect
22. accept
23. intended
24. compliment
25. thorough
26. advise
27. insurance
28. transparent
29. altogether
30. circumference
31. anchor
32. anemometer
33. persecute
34. annual
35. majority
36. hurricane
37. crocodile (others live in water)
38. camera (others are compound words)
39. artichoke (others are plural)
40. liver (others are bones)
41. tomato (others are weather conditions)
42. zipper (others have a 'double z')
43. comet
44. cabbage
45. Monday
46. Chihuahua
47. octopus
48. pajama
49. angel
50. sauerkraut
51. omelet
52. tortilla
53. molasses
54. petit fours
55. doughnut
56. spaghetti
57. j or m
58. n
59. o
60. h
61. i
62. a
63. k
64. f
65. d
66. c
67. p
68. b
69. tentacles
70. goose
71. mouse
72. freeze
73. snow
74. argument
75. surfer

STUDY & RESEARCH SKILLS TESTS ANSWER KEY

Dictionary & Encyclopedia Skills (Test on page 90)

1. 5, 3, 1, 4, 2
2. b
3. c
4. b
5. 2, 1, 3, 4, 5
6. 2, 3, 5, 1, 4
7. 1, 2, 3, 5, 4
8. 4, 3, 1, 5, 2
9. no
10. yes
11. 841
12. yes
13. 840
14. yes
15. 841
16. no
17. yes
18. no
19. yes
20. no
21. yes
22. 242
23. 841
24. no
25. 841
26. no
27. no
28. no
29. yes
30. no
31. yes
32. yes
33. no
34. Belgium
35. telescope
36. Hamlet
37. Everglades
38. verb
39. Middle English or Latin
40. 3
41. detected
42. 1
43. detectible or detectable
44. to uncover
45. ice
46. away from the sun
47. coma
48. its discoverer
49. sunlight reflects off the grains
50. dust grains and ions
    of carbon monoxide

Fifth Grade Book of Language Tests

STUDY & RESEARCH SKILLS TESTS ANSWER KEY

Reference & Information Skills (Test on page 94)

1. thesaurus
2. almanac
3. newspaper
4. dictionary
5. encyclopedia
6. book of records
7. book of quotations
8. geographical dictionary
9. atlas
10. timeline
11. biographical dictionary
12. D
13. I or J
14. N or D
15. A, G, or I
16. J or I
17. E
18. D or N
19. M
20. D
21. J or I
22. B or I
23. E or A
24. E or A
25. K or I
26. I
27. I

28. F
29. I
30. H or B
31. C
32. H
33. glossary
34. cover
35. copyright page
36. title page
37. index
38. table of contents
39. 18–25, 57–61
40. 46–67
41. Ch 3
42. 70–77
43. 93
44. 40–45 or Chapter 1
45. 6
46. 6
47. 62–67
48. 93–99
49. 54–56
50. 70–77
51. 68–99
52. 48–53 and 62–67
53. 18–45, or 26–31, 40–45, 32–39, and 18–25

54. a, d, e
55. b
56. c
57. b
58. northwest
59. Gottcha Lane
60. east
61. 5
62. missing pet boa
63. missing fingerprints
64. Anonymous Bank Deposit and Mysterious Bather or Backwards Ceremony and Missing Train
65. March and May
66. 11 (12 is also an acceptable answer)
67. 18
68. tracking
69. strange noises
70. full-time
71. Missing Pet Boa
72. Magician's Disappearance
73. 4
74. 42 (approximate answer)
75. a

Fifth Grade Book of Language Tests

STUDY & RESEARCH SKILLS TESTS ANSWER KEY

Library Skills (Test on page 100)

1. a
2. b
3. c
4. a
5. a or c or both
6. b
7. b
8. Sterling
9. yes
10. Not-So-Great Moments in Sports
11. a
12. Bears in the Wild
13. 1981
14. D. D. Tyler
15. 111
16. 700–799
17. 400–499
18. 800–899
19. 100–199
20. 900–999
21. 500–599
22. 600–699
23. 500–599
24. 200–299
25. 300–399

Study Skills (Test on page 102)

1. A, B, E, F, G, J, K (E and G are optional. They could be relevant.)
2. guests facing backwards
3. for a friend's wedding
4. diplomas
5. Main idea is something similar to this: Mr. Razer's pig mysteriously disappears and reappears.
6. A, B, D, G, H, J
7. a
8. II
9. III A
10. I B

Fifth Grade Book of Language Tests

SPELLING TESTS ANSWER KEY

Rules & Rule-Breakers (Test on page 106)

1. friend
2. weigh
3. chief
4. believe
5. grief
6. sleigh
7. neighbor
8. ceiling
9. reindeer
10. receive
11. receipt
12. veil
13–20. may be listed in any order:
syllable, necessary, different,
bananas, caterpillar, allowance,
Tennessee, scissors
21. circus
22. wrinkled
23. cough
24. celery
25. ghostly
26. sugar
27. knuckle
28. quicksand
29. whisper
30. genius
31. tomatoes
32. monkeys
33. loaves
34. messes
35. butterflies
36. geese
37. women
38. countries
39. hero
40. child
41. address
42. chef
43. wife
44. potato
45. donkey
46. echo
47. worried
48. wished
49. argued
50. froze
51. forgot
52. fought
53. tried
54. brought
55. thought
56. hitchhiker, firecracker
57. shipwreck, swimsuit, headache
58. teenager, nighttime
59. baseball
60. weird
61. ancient
62. height
63. pianos
64. noticeable
65. truly
66. neither
67. wholly
68. solos
69. pastime
70. foreign

Fifth Grade Book of Language Tests

SPELLING TESTS ANSWER KEY

Spelling with Word Parts (Test on page 108)

1. correct	19. actor	37. carrying	55. el
2. correct	20. hopeful	38. required	56. le
3. mistake	21. correct	39. slimy	57. le
4. transport	22. correct	40. giggling	58. ate
5. antibacterial	23. inconsiderate	41. echoed	59. ite
6. correct	24. irresponsible	42. carried	60. ite
7. preview	25. impossible	43. swimming	61. ate
8. correct	26. biography	44. ian	62. ate
9. department	27. disappear	45. ion	63. ish
10. submarine	28. advertisement	46. ion	64. ete
11. correct	29. accidental	47. ous	65. ize
12. correct	30. feverish	48. ous	66. ize
13. guidance	31. musical	49. ius	67. age
14. ambulance	32. imperfect	50. ant	68. edge
15. correct	33. difference	51. ant	69. age
16. possibly	34. frequently	52. ence	70. ise
17. correct	35. favorable	53. ance	
18. dentist	36. unsurprising	54. able	

Confusing & Tricky Words (Test on page 110)

1. stalk, envy, erupt	15. ou	oxygen, serious, excellent, quartet, strength, gravity, zero	32. thorough
2. carousel	16. ai		33. minors
3. mosquito	17. ou		34. dessert
4. kindergarten	18. eau		35. overdue
5. correct	19. ea	22. c	36. scared
6. tortilla	20. caterpiller, exxaggerate, circumferance, multiplacation, perpandicular, percipitation, gymnazium	23. b	37. pried
7. waffle		24. b	38. horse
8. correct		25. c	39. angles
9. correct		26. d	40. diary
10. antique		27. a	41. inspiring
11. dynamite		28. a	42. celery
12. au	21. wreath, expel, seize, apologize,	29. b	43. accept
13. oi		30. principal	44. Adopt
14. ai		31. incident	45. break

Fifth Grade Book of Language Tests

SPELLING TESTS ANSWER KEY

Correcting Spelling Errors (Test on page 112)

1. Atlantic
2. Jupiter
3. Michigan
4. Wednesday
5. Thanksgiving
6. Egypt
7. Illinois
8. Maine
9. no
10. yes
11. no
12. no
13. yes
14. no
15. yes
16. no
17. laboratory
18. twelfth
19. license
20. vegetable
21. restaurant
22. memorize
23. chocolate
24. trouble
25. vegetables, sugar, lettuce, tomatoes, noodles
26. pilot
27. people
28. caught
29. molecule
30. llama
31. laughter
32. again

33. appear
34. enough
35. separate
36. absence
37. criticize
38. weather
39. automatic
40. license
41. pianoes
42. wierd
43. notbook
44. magecal
45. subbmarine
46. terrifick
47. arithmatic
48. astronot
49–54. energy, coughed, surprise, scuba, cider, babysitter
55. tongue
56. mosquito
57. odor
58. opposite
59. ketchup or catsup
60. spinach
61. loneliness
62. tangle
63. advertise
64. Saturday
65. almost
66. because
67. toward
68. empty
69. Welcome to South

Coast National Park
70. Please Do Not Picnic After Dark
71. Hamburgers Forty Cents
72. Launch Canoes At Fifth Street Pier
73. Gasoline Straight Ahead
74. Pick up your garbage
75. Incorrect words, spelled correctly: been, desert, island, fourteen, about, whale, swallowed, know, located, half, truly
76. Freak Accidents Reported on Public Beaches
77. Doctor Does Surprise Operation
78. Ski Season Cancelled Due to Dangerous Ice Storm
79. Two Hundred Homes Lost in Tornado
80. Elephant Receives Gold Medal

Fifth Grade Book of Language Tests